ANGELS

ANGELS

MINISTERS
OF
GRACE

Geddes MacGregor

PARAGON HOUSE
NEW YORK

Published in the United States by
Paragon House
370 Lexington Avenue
New York, New York 10017

Library of Congress Cataloging-in-Publication Data
MacGregor, Geddes.
    Angels : ministers of grace.

    Bibliography.
    Includes index.
    1. Angels.   I. Title.
BT966.2.M25   1987   001.9′4   87-11243
ISBN 0-913729-42-6
    1-55778-001-3 (pbk.)

To the Very Reverend Father Cyril Molnar
Prior General of the Order of Agapē and Reconciliation
Doctor of Theology
qui angelorum socius est

CONTENTS

viii   *Contents*

ACKNOWLEDGMENTS

I wish to express my thanks to the following persons who in one way or another have helped me in my research for this book: Dr. Susan V. Lenkey, Emerita Rare Book Librarian, Stanford University, who out of her astonishing knowledge of the history of art and with her unerring judgment in the use of it selected and provided a vast number of illustrations, many of which have been used in the book; Dr. Ross Scimeca for much help, especially in the selection of the musical works mentioned in Chapter 11 and their interpretation; Mr. Rodney Rolfs, Librarian of the Music Library, University of Southern California, for a computer search of relevant works there; Mrs. Bridget Molloy, Head of the Hoose Library of Philosophy in that university, for the invaluable help she is always so ready to give with cheerfulness and grace; and in a very special way I would thank Ms. Marion Schulman, a research librarian at the same institution, whose ability to produce with almost angelic speed facts and references that had seemed all but undiscoverable evokes my astonishment as it commands my admiration.

ILLUSTRATIONS

INTRODUCTION

Angel-Talk

Everybody from time to time uses angel-talk. We use it if only to call a sleeping baby angelic. We talk of demons too: the little boys in the church choir look like angels although, we may whisper with a wry smile, they behave like little devils.

Who or what exactly are these angels and devils to which we so readily refer? Are they mere mental figments, mere poetic fancies? Could they be real entities independent of the mind?

Religious Belief in Angels

Angels are certainly a well-established part of the folklore of society both in our own Western culture and, in one form or another, in that of virtually every other culture in the world. The great religions of the world, however, not least the three great monotheistic religions (Judaism, Christianity, and Islam), traditionally take angels as seriously as they take God. This is notably true of Islam, which not only emphasizes in a special way the uniqueness, the unity, and the sovereignty of Allah but has a very definite place for angels in its system. No less is it true of the teaching of the Roman Catholic Church, whose faithful are required to recognize angels, no less than saints, as specific entities in the hierarchy of Being. In the Preface to the Canon of the Mass the celebrating priest joins "with seraphim and cherubim," "with angels and archangels," as he prepares to offer God the highest glory and praise that man can give to his Creator. Are we to say of this worship merely that it is one of the great art forms of Europe? Are the faithful who engage in it merely bemired in crass superstition and smothered in the vesture of a bygone age? Or could it be that the angels that are so confidently acclaimed might have some place in the realm of scientifically demonstrable reality?

"Science" and "Religion" in the Past

Before we can seriously consider so daring a hypothesis, we must first decide how "science" and "religion" relate to each other. Here our knowledge of the history of ideas can help us to decide for ourselves.

The classical biblical writers, for instance, made no radical distinction such as we do between these two areas. The Hebrews had no specific term for "Nature" as distinguished from "God". They wrote of what they saw as reality. They did not divide reality into areas, talking (as do we) of spiritual and physical realities, psychological and ontological realities. The Greeks did have a word for nature (*physis,* from which of course we get terms such as "physics" and "physiology"), yet the early Greek thinkers whose thought formed the cradle of Western civilization, did not make such distinctions either. The basic questions they asked about the universe might be called pseudo-scientific or pseudo-theological according to our private inclination. If, being scientifically-minded, we call their questions "primitive science," we are wrong. If, being theologically-minded, we call their questions "naive theology," we are no less wrong. For their questions antedate such distinctions and so could not have presupposed them. To ask whether they were scientific or theological questions is almost like asking whether Moses would have preferred Gothic or Palladian architecture.

How then did the distinction arise and why? The answer is likely to be very complex. It is indeed too complex to be attempted here, nor need it be. Nevertheless, we can see in the course of time a gradual recognition that the methods used in certain fields of inquiry for the pursuit of human knowledge are different from those used in others. For instance, in discovering the basic principles of elementary mechanics, people did not use exactly the same methods that were used in attempting to ascertain the best laws for governing conduct in a particular society. Astronomers and moralists both sought to understand "the way things are," but they had to approach their respective tasks differently.

People were seeing this in Europe in the twelfth century, for example, when scholars were rediscovering Aristotle, who represented "science." They saw that there seemed to be a "right way" of doing physics and a "right way" of doing theology. Indeed, so impressed were scholars by this, both in the Arab and in the

Christian world, that some talked as though there must be two different kinds of truth. *Can* there be two different kinds of truth? One, so to speak, for weekdays and the other for Sundays (or Saturday, if you are a Jew, or Friday, if a Muslim)?

One of the greatest insights attained by medieval philosophers (notably by Thomas Aquinas in the thirteenth century) is that truth must be one. That is to say, whatever differences we may be forced to recognize in the *methodologies* by which we try to ascertain truth, the truths that jurists discover in their legal studies cannot contradict truths that pathologists discover in their medical researches. The term "science" (Latin, *scientia*) means simply "knowledge" and human knowledge, if it is anything at all, is knowledge by whatever means it is attained. We may talk, as is our modern fashion, of "hard" and "soft" sciences, but if what is called true in one realm is called false in another, there must be something wrong with one finding or the other. We cannot say, for instance, that angels are "religiously true" but "scientifically false." Either one approach or the other must be modified. They must not be on a collision course.

In the thirteenth century it seemed to many scholars that Aristotle, who represented what we should nowadays call "science," was dealing a fatal blow to "religion." The genius of St. Thomas lay in his discovery that Aristotle, far from being an enemy of the Church, could be in fact her supporter and friend. As he put it in the language of his day, the "new" kind of *scientia* far from being the Church's foe, could be the *ancilla,* the handmaiden or helper, of theology. In the terms we use today he was saying, in effect, that "science" could and did enrich and clarify the meaning of what the Church was teaching.

The Concept of Evolution in Science and in Religion

In the nineteenth century something very similar occurred with the great discovery of that age: the principle of evolution. Evolutionary theories were not entirely new then, but no one before Darwin's time had amassed such an overwhelming array of evidence for it as did Darwin, Wallace, and Huxley in the biological field. Within a generation after Darwin's death in 1882 there came to the attention of the scientific world no less staggeringly convincing evidence for evolution as a general principle of the entire universe.

Scientists were seeing that the evolutionary principle is as pervasive in the development of the physical universe as it is in the development of life. *Everything* is in process. Reality lies beyond the process. For religious believers, God, as the supreme reality, the Supreme Being *(ens realissimum),* could be seen as alone beyond the realm of evolutionary process.

Of course Aristotle had seen this in his own way more than two thousand years earlier, but he had not provided (for he could not have provided) the *kind* of proof that was now coming to light. St. Thomas and Kant had seen it too, each in his own way, but within the last hundred years or so the scholarly and scientific world has come to be in a position to see it more clearly than could even such philosophical giants in their day. Since the evolutionary principle operates everywhere, "science" and "religion" cannot possibly contradict one another and at the same time give a full account of "the way things are." At some point at least one of them must modify its position and in so doing enrich its own grasp of the reality that lies beyond all human percepts and concepts of it. In so doing they act as does the snow-laden tree that exhibits the Buddhist principle of *wu-wei* by bending under the weight of the snow, which without the tree's yielding would break its branches.

"Science" and "Religion" Today

The consequences of this change of attitude in all fields of human inquiry can be seen dramatically in the reaction of biblical scholars and theologians to the evolutionary discoveries of the nineteenth century. In contrast to the reactionary attitudes of the superficially religious, theirs (even before the end of the century) took the form of a recognition that God's ways could now be seen as far more wonderful than churchmen had generally supposed. Evolution was now seen as the instrument of creation. Of course it did not prove divine creativity; it did not even purport to prove or disprove the existence of God. But to believers, it exhibited as never before something of the scale and grandeur of creation. The Bible itself was now being seen as the product of a centuries-long process of evolutionary development and revision. An ancient Greek saying was to the effect that the mills of God grind slowly but very surely. Now the learned could say, as indeed they did, that evolution is "God's way of doing things." Theological reflection had been enriched, not diminished, by scientific discovery.

Besides, in contrast to the mechanistic view of the universe that had prevailed in the eighteenth century among physicists and astronomers and had percolated into the popular attitudes of that age, inducing notions of God as a cosmic engineer, the "Grand Architect" of the universe (as though the universe were an edifice or a machine), modern scientific work has shown that, whatever the universe is, it is more like a thought than a machine. Kant (1724–1804), one of the very greatest thinkers of all time, had distinguished between the realm of "the starry heavens above" (the physical universe) and "the moral law within" (what we might call the spiritual realm), seeing a profound disparity between the methods by which the one and the other must be respectively approached. Indeed, as every scientist knows from his or her elementary studies in high school, we could make no headway even in biology by restricting ourselves to the methods of physics. Yet biology can no more contradict physics than can solid geometry contravene the "laws" of plane geometry. Theological truths, if there are any (as there must be if there is any truth in religion at all), cannot contradict "scientific" ones.

Scientific methods and discoveries are of course no more immutable than are theological ones. The hypotheses of astronomers and biochemists, when first made, can seem just as ridiculous as do the weirdest theological ones. Galileo and Pasteur were ridiculed by their contemporaries as much as (perhaps more than) any philosopher such as Berkeley or any mystic such as Boehme or Blake. In the old Indian story of the blind men and the elephant, one feels the animal's trunk and pronounces the elephant like a snake; another feels its huge leg and says the elephant is like a tree-trunk. Of course it is like both of these but very much more besides. So with God and the universe: they are much more than we can even begin to imagine. People were astonished when they learned that the universe is so vast, but the minuteness of the submicroscopic world is at least as astonishing, if not more so, than is the immensity of outer space. More astonishing still is the capacity of the three pounds of gray matter we call the human brain, which besides its merely computer-like function can attain a self-awareness and engage in self-critique beyond the abilities of even the highest of the other mammals.

In the last analysis, then, "science" and "religion" must be one, as the elephant in the old fable is one, whatever the blind men may suppose. Although the methods by which we attain human knowledge do differ, a common procedure runs through all of them: we make a hypothesis and attempt to verify or falsify it. We may make as many hypotheses as we like and as wildly as we choose, but training and experience in a particular field teach us to make hypotheses that are more likely to be profitable and not a mere waste of time. Even so, scientists generally make hundreds, even thousands of them before coming up with even a modest discovery. Religious people are said to "walk in faith," but the nature of faith is no less widely misunderstood than is the nature of scientific inquiry.

Faith and Scientific Inquiry

As we have just seen, the history of any scientific discovery is always long and arduous. Moreover, although the discovery "works" and is therefore often extremely useful, to say the least, it is not entirely conclusive. (Mathematics, being a closed system, provides an exception to this but one that does not affect the matter at hand.) That is, what is discovered is always susceptible to further inquiry and development and may have to be modified or even renounced. For instance, the geocentric theory of the universe, according to which the sun moves round the earth, primitive and arrogant though it may seem to us now, took a long time in the making. It was a necessary step to set the stage for the now accepted view of the solar system that places the sun, of course, at the center. But the discovery that the earth moves round the sun was in turn but groundwork, preliminary to what neither the genius of Copernicus nor the daring of Galileo could have discovered: that the solar system itself is a mere backwater in a tiny region of the incalculably vast universe of suns and their systems. First Copernicus, father of modern astronomy, had to overthrow a mistaken idea before the long process of further astronomical discovery could begin. Although human knowledge has indubitably advanced since their time, discovery has been by no means concluded. Indeed, scientists are continually modifying what they have learned.

Faith is likewise a long and arduous process. Far from being a mere wild, unthinking leap into a dogmatic pulpit, authentic religious faith is a process of living in such a way as to test the hypotheses suggested by one's religious disposition and so arrive at knowledge of the spiritual aspect of the universe, the dimension of Being that we identify as different from that of the tables-and-chairs world. Contrary to widespread popular misunderstanding (classically expressed in the Cockney schoolboy's definition: "believing steadfastly wot you know ain't true"), the way by which people of authentically religious disposition attain to some degree of knowledge of the spiritual dimension of Being is not by any means *entirely* different from that by which scientists arrive at their findings. It is really a descant on doubt.[1]

Both "religion" and "science" have had humble beginnings in the human spirit. Their ways at first seem similar if not the same. Then formally they must diverge, but they are in fact less divergent than is vulgarly supposed. Religious inquiry, like that of many other movements of the human spirit, requires both an introspective activity foreign to such sciences as physics and chemistry and an ontological concern such as seldom troubles scientists in their working hours; nevertheless the procedures of "science" and "religion" are surprisingly akin. Witch doctors are as misguided and primitive in their religion as they are in their science. Yet every man is a boy before becoming a man. Both "science" and "religion" proceed haltingly and neither the deeply religious person nor the original scientist ever supposes that the days of walking falteringly can end. Human knowledge of every kind is hard to win and at best is, when won, precariously held.

On Making Hypotheses, Religious or Scientific

I have dealt with these questions at some length in order to prepare the reader for a hypothesis in Part II of this book that is likely to strike some readers as startling, not to say ridiculous. I wish to forestall such prejudice against it. The hypothesis I will make suggests a scientific *possibility* that would not only accord with the belief in angels that is traditional for Christians and others who take their religion seriously, but would be scientifically plausible, however indemonstrable.

Hypotheses, unless they are entirely wild and frivolous, are a necessary first step in the long process of attempting to attain knowledge. It goes without saying that they provide no proof. Nevertheless, whether they are scientific or religious, their value lies in their being proposed not arbitrarily or flippantly but out of long, disciplined training and experience in the field to which they relate. When you feel ill, the chief value of having a good family doctor is that he or she knows, by training and experience, both the medical field in general and the particular terrain, namely, you and your body. Such a doctor, although unable to guarantee coming up with the right diagnosis on sight (i.e., the right hypothesis), is more *likely* to do so. Behind the hypothesis will be a variety of information including not only what the doctor has imbibed in medical school and acquired through many years of practice, but what he has learned about you (your body, and your mind) through having attended you as his patient. In making the diagnosis (hypothesis) the doctor, knowing that truth is one and not confined to any narrowly defined procedure, will not restrict his vision of the case to this or that kind of information. *Any* relevant information will help the doctor to make a reasonable diagnosis. Tests such as those used in modern medicine will help the doctor to discover whether the diagnosis is right or wrong. As every patient knows, the value of a good diagnostician is incalculably great, although, after all, even the best diagnosis is only a well-informed guess. Yet making it is the most basic step towards proof.

The Twofold Plan of the Present Study

The present study is divided into two parts.

In Part I our subject will be treated historically, showing the development of the concept of angels both in folklore and in theologically reflective religion.

In Part II I shall propose the following hypothesis. We know nowadays that the universe contains so incalculably great a number of galaxies each containing vast numbers of solar systems that even if not a single other planet in our own system is hospitable to intelligent life, the likelihood of such life on other planets among the trillions of possibilities is overwhelming. True, we have no empirical proof of it. We may lack such proof for a long time to come. It might even be that our planet Earth is, among all the stupendous array of others in the unthinkably immense reaches of outer space, the only one that has developed any kind of intelligent life. Theoretically it might be so, but if it were so it would be much more than ordinarily surprising, from all that we know of "the way things are." For the "laws of nature," whatever they are, are universal. They apply to Mars and every other planet in the entire universe as they apply to our own planet Earth and so, although no proof of intelligent life beyond our own planet has been established so far, the probability is so great as to make the hypothesis plausible in the most eminent degree.

If, moreover, there is intelligent life somewhere else in the universe, it is likely, from what we know of the evolutionary character of everything, that it will vary in quality as indeed it does even among us humans on this planet Earth. Some forms of such extraterrestrial life are likely to be far behind even the lowest manifestations of it on our planet and other forms of it are likely to be far more advanced than ours. What I am suggesting (as a worthwhile hypothesis but obviously no more) is that angels as they are represented in the Bible and religious tradition might be such more advanced forms of intelligent life : extraterrestrial beings who (far from being the little green men of science fiction) could have developed along another evolutionary line to a higher form than ours and be more rational, more benevolent, and so capable of helping humans in the way that angels in traditional religious lore are said to do. Speculative though the hypothesis is (and as all hypotheses must be), there is no scientific reason why it should not be a viable one and there are many indications of its plausibility. At any rate it is surely more worthwhile than is most of the angel-talk in which we commonly engage.

PART I

ANGELS
IN
FABLE
AND IN
FAITH

1

ANGELS IN POPULAR SONG AND STORY TODAY

**Angels we have heard on high
Sweetly singing through the night**
CHRISTMAS CAROL

𝕿he commercialization of Christmas brings, as we all know, plenty of trivialities and banalities. Nevertheless, in the midst of it all we may detect even there a slight flutter of angels' wings. In the city of angels, Los Angeles, dedicated in the eighteenth century to *Nuestra Señora la Reina de los Angeles* (Our Lady, Queen of the Angels) we might expect angels and we do indeed find them, of course, in abundance in forests of Christmas trees. In 1985, for instance, the Christmas tree of the Greater Los Angeles Visitors and Convention Bureau in a boutique in the Arco Towers was decorated with no fewer than two hundred angels.

Nothing so very remarkable about that, perhaps, but some of them (designed by Dom Maur van Doorslaer, a Benedictine monk of St. Andrew's Priory in the high desert just beyond the mountains to the north and handcrafted by other monks of the same community), seem to fit the popular image of Southern California which, a Christmas tree saleswoman has jocosely observed, is the only place she knows where one gets sunburnt selling trees at Christmas. For some of these angels are represented surfing, some skate-boarding, some roller-skating, some even playing tennis. The angelic assortment also includes angels created by the "Just Ducky" artists in Laguna Beach, handpainted wooden angels from East Germany,

3

glass angels from Czechoslovakia, rope ones from the Philippines, and even angels from snowbound Iowa and elsewhere in the United States. And surely it is fitting that angels should enter into such recreative joys of young people and it would certainly seem most fitting that monks of that most venerable of religious orders in the West should bring them from heaven down to earth to do so.

But who are they, these angels? No wonder popular fascination with them leads to such widespread curiosity about them.

In the mainstream of contemporary society people may not take angels very seriously, but the idea raises no eyebrows. It is very familiar, especially at Christmastide. Use of the term "angel," however, occurs in quite ordinary conversation. A thoughtful and caring nurse may be called an angel. Indeed, the word may be used of anyone as a term of endearment, almost as we use the word "darling" but generally with an overtone of special, unexpected benevolence in the person so designated.

We may call a child an angel when he or she is in a pensive or studious mood, and especially when asleep. Of course we may call a child a little devil at other times, but then a devil is an angel "gone wrong." Perhaps we have in mind those fat little cherubs of popular iconography who seem to breathe an air of nonchalant purity and innocence.

What precisely we do have in mind, however, is not by any means ever entirely clear. In the slang of the theatrical profession a person who backs a venture with money may be called an angel and there is even a verb "to angel" that is used to describe the action of so doing. The term is also used in the culinary arts. Angel food or angel cake, for instance, is a white sponge cake made of flour, sugar, and the whites of eggs. Angel pie is a baked shell of meringue filled with strawberries or other delectable fruit topped with whipped cream and served as a dessert. Oysters wrapped in bacon, skewered, and served on toast are called "angels on horseback." A long white sleeve hanging loosely from the shoulder as in a surplice or a lady's dress is sometimes called an "angel sleeve." Is there any common feature in all of these that is accounted angelic? Only, in the case of the foods, the whiteness, perhaps, and, in the case of the benefactor, the action without which the venture would not (as we sometimes say) "fly."

Everyone knows the story of Gregory the Great, who on seeing some handsome English captives offered for sale at Rome exclaimed, *"non sunt Angli sed angeli"*: they are not English but angels—an untranslatable Latin pun. But what is the quality that might evoke such a comment? Not beauty alone, surely. A beautiful girl might well be a scheming vixen and a handsome boy a vicious scoundrel. No, beauty, while it may be an ingredient in what is called angelic, is no more than an ingredient and by no means even a primary one. Purity and innocence, radiance and magnanimity, are more important elements. Above all, perhaps, is the notion of surprise and helpfulness, with the capacity to accomplish what the benevolent being intends.

Angels in Christmas carols and other popular Christmas lore seem to be so joyous that they tend to come singing. According to the Gospel for Christmas Eve (Luke 2), an angel announced to the shepherds tending their flocks by night that the Saviour of the world had been born in a stable. "And suddenly there was with the angel a multitude of the heavenly host praising God and saying, Glory to God in the highest, and on earth peace. . . ." A popular Christmas carol celebrates the beautiful story:

> Angels we have heard on high,
>   Sweetly singing through the night,
> And the mountains in reply
>   Echoing their brave delight.
>   *Gloria in excelsis deo!*

In that loveliest of Christmas carols, "Stille Nacht, Heilige Nacht," "Heavenly hosts sing alleluia." Christmas without the angels would be like Easter without sunrise. Perhaps Christmas might do without the gold and myrrh and frankincense, without the wise men and the kings, impoverished as it would be for lack of them; but one wonders whether, lacking the angels, it would be Christmas at all. Surely few Christians have not thrilled to the third stanza of "Adeste fideles":

> Sing, choirs of angels,
> Sing in exultation,
> Sing, all ye citizens of heaven above . . .

and to the refrain that seems to echo from angels in the clerestory: *Gloria in excelsis deo!*

Yet angels do not always sing. As in Phillips Brooks' beautiful Christmas hymn,

> How silently, how silently,
>   The wondrous gift is given,

so the angels in missions of mercy to the sorely afflicted often bring their benisons not with merry songs but with silent understanding. So the American Quaker poet James Greenleaf Whittier, writing to his friend on the death of a beloved sister, says:

> With silence only as their benediction
>   God's angels come
> Where, in the shadow of a great affliction,
>   The soul sits dumb.

Even in life's sorrows and tragedies may be heard, when the disguise has worn off, the flutter of angels' wings. Lowell, in a lovely poem, consoles a bereaved mother:

> But all God's angels come to us disguised:
> Sorrow and sickness, poverty and death,
> One after other lift their frowning masks,
> And we behold the Seraph's face beneath,
> All radiant with the glory and the calm
> Of having looked upon the front of God.

In everyday speech, however, angel-talk is glib. "Be an angel" can be synonymous with "Do me a favor." We talk of angels as though talking of what everybody knows about, almost as though talking of houses and gardens. The term "God" may bring anything from a half-genuflection to a skeptical giggle, depending on the company you keep. It may be used profanely along with other tepid blasphemies and mild oaths. Angels, however, do not seem to enter into such profanities, except of course the fallen ones. Is it that there lurks among even the least religious among us some vague fear of God that makes abuse of the divine name feel like an act of defiance, while angels are such friendly creatures that they simply are not fitted to function in such ways?

Creatures? We talk of sparrows and doves, of cats and dogs, as creatures, without necessarily admitting the theological implication. For the term implies a creator. But angels? Unless we are committed to some very narrow and strict form of Jewish or Christian orthodoxy we are not likely to take seriously the notion that they are created at all in the sense in which mammals and birds, insects and fish, are traditionally believed to have been created by God, each "after his kind," as the opening chapter of Genesis relates. If angels are created, are not they created by ourselves, in our own minds, as creatures of our imagination?

We shall have to consider that question much more carefully later on in this book. For the present let us simply note that *everything* that is in our mind is in some sense created by our imagination. We build up our mental images of tables and chairs in ways adapted to our human minds. I do not see the world exactly as you do, although for all practical purposes my way of apprehending the world is near enough to yours to avoid our seriously misunderstanding one another about such objects as tables and chairs. When it comes to our ways of perceiving aesthetic qualities in the world around us, however, our judgments may differ very much indeed. A French impressionist way of looking at the world may coincide with mine while a cubist way may speak more to your condition. Then do angels belong to that world of art, a real world indeed, but certainly not to be confused with the tables-and-chairs world and not even with the world that consists of "other people" such as my wife or your uncle?

Of course angels do belong to the world of art, as can be seen without going farther than the illustrations in this book. But so do you, and so do the tables and chairs, so long as there is an artist to see them with an artist's eye or a musician to hear them with a musician's ear. We *reconstruct* everything to fit the capacity of our minds. If we give wings to angels or invest them with golden hair or boy soprano voices, we are still left with the question: what ontological reality lies behind these picturesque images of ours? Rainbows come across to us as giant multicolored bows in the clouds; they are surely not like that "in themselves," but that is no reason for supposing that we invented them out of nothing but our own fertile imagination.

So Christmas or any other kind of angels, for all the pretty paraphernalia in which our imaginations clothe them, may stand for a reality beyond us. The question may be, rather, to what *kind* of an external reality might they belong?

They *might* be, for instance, our own dearest, our loved ones who have advanced to a fuller life beyond the veil of death. Such a belief, in one form or another, common in primitive societies, is also held by highly educated and intelligent men and women who have studied parapsychological phenomena. They have included in their number men such as Sir Oliver Lodge and Conan Doyle. The phenomena have been studied scientifically by the American and British societies for psychical research. So we cannot ignore the possibility that the angelic presence one may feel at one time or another, perhaps in time of great stress or poignant sorrow, might be that of a visitant such as one of these loved ones that we hold so dear. Yet neither can we exclude the possibility that it might be that of a being from another dimension of existence or even another distant planet, much further advanced in the evolutionary process than are we.

If such notions sound farfetched, let us remind ourselves (trite though the reminder may seem to many) that so in the past sounded Galileo's insistence that the earth moves round the sun, not the sun round the earth. So indeed sounded Pasteur's belief in the action of bacteria as a cause of disease. It is very unlikely indeed that angels have wings or that they are at all as they have been conventionally portrayed by painters and sculptors. Yet perhaps there may be more than mere poetic fancy in the lines of Harriet Beecher Stowe:

> Sweet souls around us watch us still,
> Press nearer to our side;
> Into our thoughts, into our prayers,
> With gentle helpings glide.

The persistent tradition to that effect that pervades so many and such different societies, from the most primitive to the most advanced, suggests that we may not be taking seriously enough the poetry about angels.

Spiritualists, however, and those who share their beliefs often talk of comparatively frequent visits by *revenants* from the other side of the veil. They may even talk of communication with them as an ongoing if not an almost continuous process. By contrast, I have rarely heard of anyone claiming such frequency among angelic visitants. On the contrary, as Robert Blair noted in the eighteenth century, angels' visits are "short and far between." It is as if they come only for very important reasons and with a specific purpose. The Angel of Death, for instance, has an obviously important mission. Angels, according to a traditional Catholic requiem prayer, come to escort the souls of the righteous to paradise. Again, they might visit one in time of extreme grief or desperate perplexity, but certainly for no trivial reason and probably not even for casual consolation.

This is suggested over and over again in the Bible itself. The shepherds who were watching over their flock by night on that first Christmas were terrified when the angel appeared to them. Why? Presumably because they knew that angels appear only on occasions of great import and may well be harbingers of some traumatic event. So the Christmas angel lost no time in reassuring the shepherds that he was the bearer of no news that would strike fear into them but, on the contrary, of news of the birth of the Saviour of the world. Then, after his brief, joyful announcement, "suddenly there was with the angel a multitude of the heavenly hosts praising God and saying, Glory to God in the highest . . ."

So angelic visitants, it would seem, are not to be confused with the spirits of the departed, although both are represented as coming to us through the stupendous power of love, which conquers all obstacles. If angels do exist as independent, real beings, they would seem to be very superior indeed. Yet what we might take to be trivial might not be trivial to them. In the realm of God's love, which they manifest, nothing that loves can be trivial.

2

ANGELS IN CATHOLIC TRADITION

Angels and ministers of grace defend us!

SHAKESPEARE, *HAMLET*

Even among the most devout of Christians and the most observant of Jews today, men and women who profess deep faith in God, the concept of angels does tend to sound farfetched, not to say fanciful. Yet it is one that so permeates the Bible that even the most casual onlooker with no axe to grind either for or against any particular religious outlook must wonder how anyone whose faith has any biblical roots at all can set aside what is such an integral part of biblical teaching, to say nothing of the spiritual experience of people of every age and religious tradition.

Protestants, whose Reformation heritage claims in a special way such biblical roots, often talk almost glibly of God and of Jesus Christ as his only-begotten Son and even (despite the intellectual difficulties) of the Trinity; yet many of them habitually avoid the notion of unseen beings, messengers of God and instruments of his grace, as though it were no more than an echo of bygone superstition, an embarrassment to mature faith in God.

In Catholic tradition, as in Eastern Orthodoxy, angels are regularly invoked as part of the liturgical scenario. In the Preface to the most solemn part of the Mass, the celebrating priest joins the entire community of believers on earth with that of "all the company of heaven" and specifically unites himself and all the faithful around

10

him with angels and archangels, with seraphim and cherubim, who ceaselessly adore and praise God, crying *Sanctus, sanctus, sanctus.* Traditionally (although Vatican II has modified the practice), sacramental confession is made to God in the presence of the archangel Michael, Prince of the Angels. Moreover, a popular devotion that had begun at least as early as the fourteenth century and came into general use in the seventeenth is called the *Angelus,* after the opening words: "The angel of the Lord declared unto Mary." This devotion must have imbued the minds of millions with the reality not only of the angel Gabriel who announced to Mary the forthcoming conception and birth of Christ but of the wonder of a dimension of existence that is peopled by the unseen hosts of angelic beings who function as intermediaries between God and his people. The *Angelus* devotion is beautifully represented in the painting by Jean-François Millet in the Louvre, showing a French peasant couple having halted their work in the fields to stand with heads bowed in prayer in an attitude of simple dignity and profound reverence at the sound of the midday Angelus bell.

Yet even Catholics, accustomed as they are in their regular devotions to the invocation of Mary and the saints, seem to find themselves less comfortable, to say the least, in talk of angels. Saints seem nearer and more familiar; angels are too distant from the daily concerns of men and women. Saints, after all, have been embodied in flesh and blood like the rest of us; they have known the joys and sorrows of human life; they have passed through birth and death. The Church has officially honored them (or, rather, some of them) because they have excelled in the human pilgrimage. So, heroes and heroines though they be, they are still our fellows, who understand what it is to be hungry and tired and ill and in pain and to suffer all the other trials that human beings are called upon to endure. Angels, by contrast, are, according to medieval tradition, "separate intelligences" unencumbered by bodies such as ours and able to operate, therefore, with inconceivable speed, faster than the speed of light, whose special nature the Church Fathers had in their own way in some measure detected and used in analogy with the interior illumination of the spirit of man. So, even to the devout, angels can seem a little remote.

Indeed, although the Roman Catholic Church requires of all its members a belief in the existence of angels as an essential part of Church teaching, one may well ask how many Catholics ever give it a thought. Probably very few do, even among the most devout, practicing Catholics who habitually, in their prayers, invoke Mary and the saints. Even the Pope (John Paul II), when he visited Ireland on Michaelmas Day, made no allusion to angels! What may be even more astonishing is that probably very few noticed the fact. Yet if angels had been taken seriously, the Pope's coming to Ireland on Michaelmas Day and saying nothing about the Archangel Michael would have astonished Ireland almost as much as if he had arrived there on the seventeenth of March and failed to mention Saint Patrick.[1] The reason for the difference is the one we have already noted: it is not that today Catholics believe in the saints but not in angels; it is simply that angels do not normally enter into the Catholic imagination as do saints. Nevertheless, as we shall presently see, angels have played a very important role in Catholic art, although popular devotion has generally put them at best on its back burner. The average well-instructed Catholic, if asked what the *Angelus* was about, would probably say it was a devotion in honor of Mary. Of course the answer would be technically correct, although the angel Gabriel who brought the supremely good news to humankind would have been relegated to the role of a celestial mailman.

Yet despite the fact that Catholic piety is generally more comfortable with the saints than with the angels, there is of course a firm place for them in the Church's teaching, which finds expression in art and devotion. Their existence is *de fide* for the Church and their place in Catholic piety is assured, since Catholic faith and practice are grounded in the Bible, which is no less authoritative for Catholics than for Protestants although the attitudes of the two traditions differ in the way in which they respectively treat the relation of Bible to Church.

In the first centuries of the Christian era, when the Church was emerging in a polytheistic environment, caution was necessary in the encouragement of devotion to the angels, since it was likely to be interpreted as implying a belief in a plurality of gods. Origen, in his treatise against Celsus, affirms that Christians do not adore angels but nevertheless revere them *(therapeuein) (Contra Celsum,* VIII, 13). Augustine similarly insists that Christians lovingly revere angels but do not worship them *(De vera religione,* 55, 110).[2] As Christianity established itself, however, such caution seemed increasingly unnecessary. At Constantinople, after the time of Constantine, some fifteen churches were dedicated to the Archangel

Michael. By the time of Gregory the Great in the sixth century, devotion to the angels had a center on Monte Gargano. From the eighth century, Mont Saint-Michel, which has to this day remained one of the greatest of Christian shrines, became the center of devotion to the Archangel Michael. In the ninth century, Rome had seven oratories dedicated to him.

That such devotion to the angels was fostered by the Benedictine tradition is suggested in Chapter 19 of the founder's Rule, which, in enjoining his monks to observe a very special reverence in saying or singing the long "Divine Office" *(divinum officium)* together daily, reminds them that it is to be performed in the presence and sight of God and his angels. Bernard of Clairvaux (1090–1153), a principal representative of Benedictine spirituality in its primitive simplicity, particularly fostered devotion to the angels. In the sixteenth century, Ignatius of Loyola, no doubt in reaction against the Protestant Reformers who repudiated devotion both to saints and to angels, urged members of his Society, the Jesuits, to imitate the purity of the angels in the conduct of their lives. Both Francis Borgia and Francis Albertini wrote treatises on devotion to the angels and Cardinal Bérulle contributed to the promulgation of such devotion.

The characteristic representation of angels in Christian iconography seems to have been determined as early as the end of the second or beginning of the third century, about which time is dated a fresco of the Annunciation conserved in the cemetery of Priscilla in the Via Salaria in Rome (one of the oldest of the catacombs). Here the angel appears as a human figure, youthful, unbearded, clothed in white. Generally following the same imagery, angels are found extensively in Christian art from an early date, sometimes as messengers or guardians or guides, especially in funerary contexts, but also as assistants at the Throne in scenes depicting Jesus or Mary in majesty. Adoring angels are depicted on the triumphal arch of the Basilica of Saint Paul on the Ostian Way, dating from the fifth century. From the twelfth century, and more especially from the thirteenth, artists and sculptors began to show a greater tendency to let their fancy run freely.

In Christian iconography angels are traditionally represented in ways that make them easily identifiable; nevertheless, the symbolism varies considerably. They are usually winged. The wings symbolize the readiness to fulfil the divine command with the utmost speed. They may carry a pilgrim's staff, which likewise symbolizes readiness. They are frequently shown as handsome young men, barefooted and attired in a long tunic, but may be represented as beautiful young women. If shown as men they may sometimes be wearing a priest's stole, sometimes an archbishop's pallium. They may wear a girdle or cincture round the waist: another symbol of readiness and dedication to their angelic mission.

When they are depicted in an attitude of adoration they may carry a thurible (representing prayer) or a musical instrument (representing praise). If victory is the theme, they will probably be bearing a palm, symbol of victory, while if the theme is purity they will probably carry a lily. (These symbols may refer to the persons to whom they have been sent or whom they conduct to heaven.) They may also carry a trumpet, signifying their function as the voice of God, or a flaming sword, signifying his righteous judgment, or a scepter signifying God's kingship.

Where the various orders and choirs of angels are to be represented, this is generally accomplished in certain traditional ways, often making identification quite easy. There are three orders with three choirs in each. In descending order of rank they are as follows and are traditionally so represented:

(1) The *Seraphim,* following the biblical description (Isaiah 6), are shown with six wings and flames of fire around them, for they are "fiery spirits." They may bear a shield emblazoned with the words "Holy, holy, holy is the Lord of Hosts" *(Sanctus, sanctus, sanctus, Dominus Deus Sabaoth).* They are led by Uriel.

(2) The *Cherubim* are frequently depicted with multi-eyed peacock's feathers, to symbolize their "all-knowing" character. Their leader is Jophiel.

(3) The *Thrones* are represented as wheels of fire. They are the throne-bearers of God, symbolizing the divine majesty. They are led by Japhkiel.

These first three angelic choirs together compose the order closest to God. They are followed by the next order of three choirs, the priest-princes of the court of heaven. These usually wear albs with green or golden stoles, golden girdles, and sometimes scepter and crown. They are:

(4) The *Dominations* who, under the leadership of Zadkiel, carry scepter and sword to symbolize the divine power over all creation.

(5) The *Virtues* who, under the leadership of Haniel, carry the instruments of the Passion of Christ.
(6) The *Powers,* who carry a flaming sword because they are the protectors of humankind. Their leader is Raphael.
Last come the ministering angels as follows:
(7) The *Principalities* who, under Chamael, are the protectors of princes and usually carry sword, scepter, and cross.
(8) The *Archangels,* under Michael.
(9) The *Angels,* that is, those who have none of the above special ranks or commissions in the celestial army.

The embodiment of angels in human form, winged or otherwise, is of course an iconographic device. Origen attributed to them an ethereal or "subtle" body and Augustine seems inclined so to view them; but Christian theologians generally and the medieval school-men in particular have stressed their incorporeal nature, no doubt partly in an effort to dispel imagery based upon the crudities of popular belief. In the Aristotelian framework of medieval scholasti-cism, the concepts "material" and "immaterial" were used rigidly in a way that discouraged if it did not preclude speculation about embodiments finer than our human flesh-and-blood kind. Such "subtle" embodiments have nevertheless, as we have seen, some warrant in Scripture as well as in the ancient wisdom generally. Moreover, if Christ be risen, as of course Catholic doctrine insists, then his resurrection surely implies an embodiment of some kind. If Catholics are to take at all seriously the corporeal Assumption of Mary, then she, too, must have some sort of embodiment. Since she is hailed as "Queen of the Angels" it would certainly seem theolog-ically fitting that they should be embodied too. At any rate, apart from philosophical and scientific difficulties about disembodied spirits, the notion that such disembodied entities should be under the reign of an embodied celestial queen would seem from every point of view difficult, not to say unintelligible.

Shakespeare was, to say the least, near enough to England's medieval Catholic heritage to make Hamlet exclaim, on seeing his father's ghost, "Angels and ministers of grace defend us!" Ghosts, the spirits of the dead, are too alarming to be dealt with by any human agency. They demand the intervention of angels. Yet this language that Hamlet uses cannot be said to have been, and certainly is not now, typical of Catholic utterance. It reflects, rather, an underground influence within the main current of European thought: an influence that the Pseudo-Dionysius (*fl.* A.D. 500) may have bequeathed to the Church but which the Church somehow never quite knew how to handle as well as it handled the saints in popular devotion.

If all that be true of the devout, what of the millions on the fringe of religious faith, the half-skeptics and others who can barely entertain belief in God and who look with misgiving or worse on all religious ideas as the inventions of crafty priests for their own aggrandizement and the plenishing of their own pockets? To them the notion of angels is of course as alien as the nostrums of the witch doctor. They quote with glee, as the ultimate in absurdity, a question supposedly asked by some schoolman in the late, decadent period of the Middle Ages: "How many angels can dance on the point of a pin?"[3] If, however, we are to believe in anything beyond whatever we may choose to account the bare empirical data, surely we must recognize that the notion of a realm of beings beyond us and capable of exerting influence upon us (perhaps some in beneficent, others in maleficent ways) is as plausible as belief in God, to say nothing of the paraphernalia of religion that "goes with the territory" not only of the Church but of the more generally accepted outlook of educated opinion today.

Before we pursue any such philosophical questions, however, let us look at the role of angels in the Bible and what that most influential of literatures has to say about their nature and function. The biblical writers, although they knew nothing of modern sciences and technology, shared with the other men and women of their day a spiritual awareness that has been widely lost today. After all, if somewhere along the evolutionary path of our biological history we can lose the sense of smell that dogs and other animals so keenly possess to their great advantage, is it so unlikely that we may have lost an infinitely more precious awareness of a realm of being as invisible to our bodily eyes as that of the submicroscopic world of modern physics, yet of even greater importance for our mental health and our spiritual vitality? Few educated people today rule out completely the *possible* existence of superior intelligences on other planets in other galaxies. Why, then, should people, not least those who profess belief in God and that "God is a spirit," reject out of hand a traditional belief in an order of beings superior to us?

1. THE CELESTIAL CHORUS.
Giotto di Bondone (1266–1337), *Last Judgement*. Cappella dell'Arena, Padua.

2. LOOK, TOBIT, GRAB THE FISH! (Tobit 6.3).
H. van Rijn Rembrandt (1600–1669), *Tobias Is Shown Fish*. Pen and ink
drawing. Rijksmuseum, Amsterdam.

3. QUICK, PETER, ESCAPE AND RUN!
Raphael Sanzio (1483–1520), *Liberation of St. Peter*. Wall painting, Vatican.

4. MICHAEL BALANCING SOULS.
Roger van der Weyden (1400–1464), *Last Judgement*. Beaune, France.

5. A MODERN MICHAEL AT COVENTRY.
Sir Jacob Epstein (1880–1959).
Bronze sculpture. Coventry Cathedral, England.

6. MARY IN AWE OF GABRIEL.
Simone Martini (1283–1344), *Annunciation*. Siena.

7. MARY GREETED BY GABRIEL.
   Fra Angelico (1387–1455), *Annunciation*. Prado, Madrid.

8. GABRIEL IN AWE BEFORE THE QUEEN OF HEAVEN.
Leonardo da Vinci (1452–1519), *Annunciation*. Uffizi, Florence.

9. DEVIL CARRYING OFF A WOMAN TO HELL.
Luca Signorelli (1441–1523), *The Last Judgment*. Orvieto Cathedral,
Cappella di San Brizio.

10. CHERUBIM IN HEAVENLY GRANDEUR.
Late 10th century Ottonian miniature from Commentary, Bamberg Staatsbibliothek, Germany.

11. CHERUBS FROLICKING IN ST. PETER'S.
Gianlorenzo Bernini (1598–1680), Holy Water stoup. St. Peter's, Rome.

3

ANGELS IN THE BIBLE

The truth is they [angels] are all spirits whose work is service, sent
to help those who will be the heirs of salvation. . . . He did not
appoint angels to be rulers of the world to come, and that world is
what we are talking about.

HEBREWS 1:14 AND 2:5 (JERUSALEM BIBLE)

The English word "angel" is a
transcription of the Greek word *aggelos,* which in turn translates
the Hebrew *mal'ak,* meaning "messenger." In the Bible, however,
angels are not only messengers; they constitute the court of heaven.
In Hebrew the word is sometimes used with the addition of *Yahweh*
or *Elohim:* "the angel of the Lord" or "the angel of God." In some
later books (e.g., in Job 5:1; Ps. 89:6, 8; Daniel 8:13) angels appear
as God's retinue. They are even called *benē elōhim,* God's sons,
and, in Greek, *hoi hagioi,* "the holy Ones." We must remember that
the Hebrews had a polytheistic background and that even when
they became strictly monotheistic they may have had a residual
need to do something with the old pantheon. By displacing the
gods of the past and replacing them with angels they could not
only preserve the central concept of God as One; they could fit the
old gods, as psychological archetypes, into their newer way of
thinking without detriment to ingrained mental habit. (Later on, in
the development of Christianity, the saints were to function similarly.) In Genesis 6:1–4 occurs a strange allusion to explain the
origin of heroes: as the human race multiplied, certain angels, "the
sons of God," were attracted to "the daughters of men," and had
sexual union with them. This reflects a notion that has counterparts

25

in Greek and other primitive folklore in which mortal women are seduced by immortal gods. Such primitive notions recede as polytheistic habits of mind fade; but echoes remain. More will be said of this notion in Chapter 6.

In Genesis 19 two visitors who come to Lot to warn him and his family of the approaching destruction of Sodom and Gomorrah are designated angels. (In Hebrews 13:2 we are told that "some people have entertained angels without knowing it.") In Genesis 22:11 it is "an angel of the Lord" who stays the hand of Abraham to prevent his slaying his beloved son Isaac as a sacrificial offering to God. In Exodus 3:2 Moses sees an angel "in the shape of a flame of fire" in the burning bush. In Genesis 28:12 ff., we read of Jacob's dream in which he saw a ladder from heaven to earth on which angels were climbing up and down: a ladder that Francis Thompson, using modernized imagery, was to call "pitched between heaven and Charing Cross."

When we hear so much talk of angels in the Bible, we naturally wonder how the Hebrew people really thought of them. Did they take them to be "pure spirits" or somehow embodied? Why are they there at all? What is their nature? Of course angels have an obvious role in monotheistic religions such as Judaism, Christianity, and Islam: they are needed as a means of communication from God to man. They are trumpets through which the voice of God is heard. Beyond that, however, we cannot hope to extract from the Bible any clear notion of how the biblical writers conceived them. In Isaiah's vision (Isaiah 6) they are described in poetic detail, some with six wings, each pair with a function of its own; but that is plainly poetic symbolism. The Hebrews, especially in the classical period, were not much given to philosophical analysis or speculation. They were too preoccupied with the everyday problems of eking out a living from the inhospitable land to have time or inclination for such intellectual enterprises.

So in some passages (e.g., Hebrews 1:14) they are called "spirits," suggesting the incorporeal nature that the great thirteenth-century thinker St. Thomas later assigned to them, while in other passages they would seem to be understood as having some kind of embodiment. In Luke 20:36, Jesus is reported as saying that we human beings, after our resurrection, are to be "like the angels" *(isaggeloi)* and since we are to have an embodiment of some kind in the resurrected state, however transfigured it may be, he seems clearly to imply that angels too have an embodiment. That the angels have a nature similar to man's and differ from him only in the degree of their perfection is suggested by Jesus in his application of Ps. 82:6 in John 10:34–37. Angels seem to be conceived as beings such as men and women might become if they were to rise above their present, sin-trapped condition and realize their spiritual nature in its plenitude. Yet the Bible provides no clear angelology.

The notion that angels are beings whose nature we share, although in an undeveloped way, runs counter to the medieval scholastic tradition in which even the beatified saints in heaven are of a different order of being from the angels. The schoolmen, no less than the ancients, did not think in evolutionary terms as we must think today. Only when ancient and medieval writers try to formulate a theory about angels do they develop notions of their being a totally separate order of creation. When they did try to make such formulations they generally accounted the angels a higher order of being, as humanity is a higher order than are horses and dogs.

In Islam, however, we find a special view of the fall of the angels. According to the Qur'ān (*sūra* XX, 116), the angels were created before man. When man was then created as the supreme handiwork of God, the angels were enjoined to bow down before man: an order that prompted Lucifer's rebellion and that of his cohorts, resulting in their fall.[1] In Christian tradition, however, angels have been generally presumed to be a higher order of being than man. The Bible, moreover, by its very lack of the enunciation of any clear view of the status of angels, is open to an interpretation that would accord better with our modern evolutionary understanding of the universe in which, since we see humanity rooted in lower forms of life, we cannot easily exclude the notion that there must be higher forms of life (whether on other planets in far-off galaxies or in dimensions of existence beyond our empirical reckoning) toward which we are slowly rising. St. Thomas, in his own way, perceived more than 700 years ago that we humans cannot be the highest beings in the created order.

As already noted, angels in the Bible are more than messengers. They surround the Throne of God. The notion of an entourage of adoring angels is one that would come naturally to a people who had adopted the symbolism of God as king and supreme potentate. Some of the features of this imagery may have been derived from foreign, possibly Mesopotamian or Persian, sources, but the model is already there in Israel itself. The other role of angels as messengers or ambassadors of the divine is one that seems virtually indispensable in a severely monotheistic religion. Angels serve as intermediaries between God and the prophets. As the Hebrews, through the influence of these prophets, became more and more strictly monotheistic, the need for angels as messengers would become more and more obvious. Christianity inherited that need, despite the centrality of Christ as Mediator, and in Islam angels play a very notable role indeed.

In the Wisdom and apocalyptic literatures, angels figure prominently. Tobit refers to Raphael, Uriel, and Jeremiel by name. Raphael assists Tobit and his sons in their needs. He is mentioned as one of the seven angels who present the prayers of the saints to God (Tobit 12:15). This theme is echoed in the Apocalypse (Revelation 8:2 ff.).

Daniel is the only book in the Hebrew canon that mentions angels by name: Gabriel and Michael. In Daniel they have the function of watchers. The creation of angels is referred to in the Book of Psalms (Ps. 148:2, 5) and the New Testament has an allusion to it too (Colossians 1:16).

As we have seen, angels are frequently mentioned in the Torah itself, though not named. The Talmud alludes to four archangels around the Throne of God: Michael is at the right, Gabriel at the left, Uriel in front, and Raphael behind. It is Uriel who brings the light of knowledge of God to men; hence, presumably, his position. The Mishnah, however, makes no mention of them and some talmudic rabbis are similarly silent on the subject. This attitude seems to be not only carried over to but emphasized in the Haggadah, the Passover liturgical text, which explicitly and contrary to the Torah (Exodus 14:19; see also 23:20) states that the deliverance from Egypt was accomplished *directly* by God. Nevertheless, in some Jewish traditions much is made of the angels. The Merkā-bah mystics, for instance, as we shall see later, claim to meet angels at various stages in their mystical ascent toward the Throne of God.

There is an explicit reference to evil angels in the Book of Psalms (Ps. 78:49) and Saul was troubled by an evil spirit (I Samuel 16:14). We shall consider the notion of evil angels further in our next chapter. For the present we focus on the benevolent ones in the various functions the Bible assigns to them.

Angels are inseparable from the New Testament. They attend both the prediction of the birth of Christ (Luke 1:22–38) and the birth itself (Luke 2:9–14). They minister to Christ both after his great temptation (Matthew 4:11) and in his agony in Gethsemane (Luke

22:43). They declare his resurrection and ascension (Matthew 28:2; John 20:12; Acts 1:10 ff.). They are so much a part of the scenario and of the unfolding drama of the life of Christ as recorded in the Gospels that any attempt to read these without them would be almost like trying to understand medieval art without the Catholic faith that inspired it. They are reported as watching over Christ's "little ones" (Matthew 18:10), as rejoicing over a contrite sinner (Luke 15:10), as present when Christians worship together (I Corinthians 11:10), and as bringing prayer before God (Revelation 8:3 ff.). They carry the souls of the redeemed into paradise (Luke 16:22). They are even associated with the Last Judgement(e.g., Matthew 13:39, 41; 16:27; 24:31).

In the Book of Acts, which is presented as a straightforward historical account of the doings of the early Christians as seen through believers' eyes, angels appear no less habitually. An angel releases Peter and John from prison (Acts 5:19) and directs Philip on the road to Gaza (8:26). The writer of Acts reminds his readers (23:8) that the Sadduccees do not believe in angels, while the Pharisees do. Paul, in a dream, is visited by an angel who assures him that all on the ship will be saved (27:23). The Apocalypse or Book of Revelation is so permeated with references to angels that the casual reader might almost suppose it to consist of a treatise on their activities. One cannot easily profess to revere the Bible and dim out angels as an irrelevant superstition detachable from the rest of the text. However we may understand them, they are an inextricable part of the biblical scenery.

4

GOOD AND EVIL AGENCIES IN BIBLICAL AND GNOSTIC LITERATURE

For it is not against human enemies that we have to struggle, but against the Sovereignties and the Powers who originate the darkness in this world, the spiritual army of evil in the heavens.

EPHESIANS 6:12

We have already seen hints in the New Testament that everyone is attended by invisible helpers of one kind or another. Not only do such ministering spirits watch over the "little ones" (Matthew 18:10); they attend the individual members of the Body of Christ, providing guidance and aid (Hebrews 1:14). Beliefs of this sort existed in Jewish thought and are expressed, for example, in Enoch 100:5,[1] although they are not clearly enunciated in the Hebrew canon. In the Mediterranean world, however, they are common. In pre-Christian Roman religion every man had his Genius, every woman her Juno. Plato refers to such a belief in Greece (*Phaedo* 108 B). There is an echo of it in Acts 12:15. The Shepherd of Hermas, a book that is included in some of the most ancient of extant biblical manuscripts and one that might very well have found a permanent place in the New Testament canon, claims to have been at least in part revealed to Hermas (c. A.D. 140–155) by an angel in the shape of a shepherd. It explicitly states that every man has both a good angel to guide him and a wicked one who tries to seduce him into evil (Shepherd, Mandate VI, 2).[2]

The early Fathers of the Church were not unanimous, however, in their view on this subject. Jerome held that sin can drive away one's guardian angel, while Ambrose taught that the righteous are expressly deprived of their guardian angels in order that they may attain greater moral strength and finer spiritual quality by achieving their goal independently, *without* benefit of such external aid: an interesting belief that reflects the same kind of emphasis on the purity of free choice as is found in Stoic philosophy and in some of the presuppositions behind the ancient Upanishadic view of the nature of individual freedom under the karmic principle. It may also have some affinities with the notion of periods of spiritual drought that affect the lives of the saints, according to the testimony of Christian mystical writers: a notion that has roots not only in Hermas (*Vision* III, 9.3) but even in the *akēdia* mentioned in the Septuagint itself (e.g., Ps. 119:28 equals Ps. 118 in the Septuagint). For although this spiritual drought is commonly presented as having a negative connotation suggesting malaise and weariness, it also has a challenging function that could be interpreted as that of facing life's problems utterly alone: the classic notion of the sense of the absence of God in which God is better known than in his presence.

Honorius of Autun, in the twelfth century, was perhaps the most definite of the medieval Christian writers in teaching that each soul, in the very instant of its being embodied, is entrusted to the protection of a guardian angel.[3] In the following century both Thomas and Scotus accepted the concept of the guardian angel. Thomas held that only angels of the lowest rank are appointed to this office, while Scotus taught that one might be guarded by any member of any order of angels.[4]

We must now ask, however, a basic question: against what are these guardian angels guarding us? It is impossible to understand what the New Testament writers say about angels without first recognizing the Gnostic background of their thought. When Paul and others talk of "angels" and "principalities" and "powers" (e.g., Romans 8:38 ff.; I Corinthians 15:24, 26; Colossians 1:16; Ephesians 1:21; 3:10; I Peter 3:22), they may have been thinking of star-spirits: the "elemental spirits" *(stoicheia),* as Paul calls them (Galatians 4:3, 9; see also Galatians 4:10; Colossians 2:8, 20; Ephesians 6:12). All this imagery springs from distinctly Gnostic motifs that are to be found in late pre-Christian Judaism and plainly influenced the thought of at least some of the New Testament writers, not least Paul and John. When John talks of Satan as the "ruler of this world"

(John 12:31; 14:30; 16:11) and Paul calls him "the god of this world" (II Corinthians 4:4), they are using Gnostic language and they are thinking in a Gnostic way.

The language is appropriate for the expression of their understanding of what the Christian message is; otherwise they would not use it. That does not mean that they subscribe to everything that Gnosticism had to say. That would have been mentally impossible, for Gnosticism took as many forms as does existentialism today and there is no more reason to expect them to subscribe to all forms of Gnosticism than there would be for expecting Sartre or Camus to subscribe to everything Kierkegaard said. Nevertheless, they plainly think in Gnostic terms and accept the Gnostic scenario. What the New Testament writers assert, in one way or another, is that Christ is "the head of every principality and power."

This theocentric and christocentric insistence changes the focus, putting everything into a new perspective in which the Christian proclamation *(kerygma)* can be and is fearlessly and joyfully uttered. Christ is Lord of the *kosmos* and exalted above every other possible power in the spiritual realm; but the existence of these other powers, these "angels," far from being denied, is recognized as a fundamental reality. The writer to the Ephesians, in urging them to grow "strong in the Lord" so as to be "able to resist the Devil's tactics," gives an explicit reason for the need for such superhuman strength: we are not struggling against human enemies but "against the Sovereignties and the powers who originate the darkness in this world, the spiritual army of evil in the heavens" (Ephesians 6:10–12). In plain modern words one could say: "You need no longer be afraid of the evil eye or of 'things that go bump in the night.' "

In spite of such language and the immense and important recent research that has been done by contemporary scholars on Gnosticism, the mystery religions, and other religious phenomena in the Mediterranean world in the first century, one still hears denials that Paul and others of his time could have been thinking of demons or evil angels when they talked of Sovereignties and Powers *(hai archai kai hai exousiai)*. Some claim that they were thinking, rather, of earthly powers that impede or lie in the way of the triumph of God. Wesley Carr, for instance, takes such a view in *Angels and Principalities,*[5] on the ground that Gnosticism was not a significant force in Paul's time, so that to attribute to Paul a preoccupation with evil agencies that might be called Satan's cohorts is anachronistic.

On the contrary, if recent New Testament scholarship has shown us anything at all, it is that Gnostic ideas of one sort or another were very much in the background of even the earliest of the New Testament writers. Failure in the past to recognize this was a major impediment to an understanding of the New Testament. Because Gnosticism became a problem for the Church in the second century, conventional scholars in the past took it to have been a comparatively new development. On the contrary, it was present in the Mediterranean world long before it developed in the way and to the extent that so vexed the Church about the middle of the second century.

From the Dead Sea Scrolls found in 1947 at Qumran we learn that the community there who had followed the "Teacher of Righteousness" before and during the time of Jesus was much preoccupied with the notion of a war between the "Sons of Darkness" and the "Sons of Light." This characteristically Gnostic, dualistic motif is abundantly clear in the documents that have been retrieved in that great manuscript discovery. The Qumran community apparently believed that the forces of good and evil were working with equal force like two great armies pitted against each other and locked in conflict, but the time would come when a decisive battle would be won and Michael, as leader of the Sons of light, would lead his side to victory. The members of the community seem to have viewed themselves as having been appointed to serve in a special way in that final battle against Satan. They thought of themselves as ready to be organized under the leadership of groups of angels who were to be in charge of specific military engagements in that great conflict.

The Qumran documents everywhere reflect the Jewishness of their background, but it is a distinctive genre of Jewish mysticism in which angels play a distinctive role. The imagery comes straight out of the classical Hebrew prophets, but the use to which they are put shows how the community had been imbued with typically Gnostic ideas, including a strong emphasis on a spiritual conflict that is going on in a realm or dimension above us between angelic forces, good and evil. The imagery, for example, of the "Throne Chariot" of God is familiar to all who know the Book of Ezekiel; but along with an emphasis on the supremacy of God is developed the theme of a superhuman spiritual warfare conducted by angelic warriors.

The theme of a war between the angels persisted long after

Gnosticism has ceased to be the pervasive, not to say fashionable, influence it was in New Testament times. After the Church had pushed open manifestations of that outlook underground it continued to flourish, often below the surface and in secret groups, but sometimes emerging quite openly, having been smuggled, so to speak, from crypt to nave. It has done so right down to our own time. The Qumran documents and other such recent discoveries have revived an interest that was already well established in the religious consciousness of Europe and not hard to find if one knew where to look. Sometimes one did not have to look far, for it was staring one in the face with the boldness of a *chef de cuisine* who had suddenly emerged from the kitchen and had come to see how the guests at the banquet were enjoying what he had prepared.

I vividly recall, for example, during a prolonged stay in Paris in 1951, seeing a performance, in the evening of July 10th, of a medieval morality play, *Le Vray Mystère de la Passion,* out of doors, on the Parvis de Notre Dame. The façade of the great cathedral formed the backdrop. While the actors on the ground below were presenting us with a lively play in which they acted out a simple story of the embroilments and follies in which we humans customarily engage, our eyes were drawn upwards to the scene far above in which Lucifer and the Archangel Michael, darting in and out of parapets and gargoyles, were engaged in a heavenly sparring match. As they fought it out, each deftly succeeding now and then in surprising his adversary with a rapier thrust and each from time to time slipping out of sight with no less dexterity, one became quickly aware that however amusing might be the antics of the players below, engaged as they were in the petty squabbles of human life, the real warfare was being conducted far above them.

The players' intentional obliviousness to it was strikingly convincing, for physically they could not see it, while we, the audience, could. We were being let in, so to speak, on the secret of the angels. We were privileged to see before our very eyes where the action was: the real action. It was not going on down there among the human participants who were so preoccupied with what they would have called "the real world" that they looked, and were intended to look, as though they knew of nothing else going on outside their little flat rectangle of pavement. The real action, however, was not going on "down there" at all but "up there" in the Gothic turrets. The people down below seemed like mere pawns, if not puppets, in the war being waged on high.

What came across so impressively was that even as we humans glue our eyes to the scenes of everyday life and pride ourselves in our involvement with whatever society we find around us, we conduct even our bitterest feuds, even indeed our global wars, with blinkers over our eyes, with tunnel vision that precludes our having even a hint of awareness of the real warfare that is going on, of which ours is a mere feeble reflection, like the shadows cast on the ground by squadrons of aircraft engaged in combat above us. How ludicrous and pathetic we must be with our inward-looking engagements for war and solemn assemblies for peace, if war is being waged by the heavenly hosts between the Angels of Light and the Angels of Darkness, while we plod our way through the mud, following like children the shadow-boxing images their warfare is casting on the ground!

No New Testament scholar has more clearly exhibited the presence and importance of such Gnostic motifs in the canonical writers than has Rudolf Bultmann. He has shown in many ways the preoccupation with such ideas in the first-century Church. The question is not at all whether there were such motifs, but what kinds of Gnosticism were accepted and what kinds were repudiated. As I have shown elsewhere, there is a striking parallel not only between Gnosticism and modern existentialism, but between the predicament of the first-century Church in this regard and that of the twentieth-century Church in respect to modern forms of existentialism.[6] Some of these are patently antithetical to any view that could be called religious in even the loosest sense, while others are so strikingly expressive of the Christian outlook that they have deeply influenced Christians of the most varied traditions in our own times.

Bultmann, one of the most eminent New Testament scholars of our time, specifically calls attention to the realm of angels (principalities, powers, and other agencies in the cosmos) as an arena of conflict and of resistance in the Church. Why? One important reason is that the canonical writers are concerned to show Christ as Lord of all principalities and powers. Within the Church, however, were many who, under Gnostic influence, seem to have been too much preoccupied with what they took to be an ongoing war between good and evil agencies and this view was resisted on the ground that, in effect, Christ had won that war in the sense that those who trusted in him could put the evil demons to flight by invoking his name. Bultmann suggests that the Gnostics that were deprecated were those who were thinking of the angel-world as primarily "a realm of enemy powers" whom they could and must fight with their esoteric knowledge. The canonical writers resisted such notions because they implied a dualism contrary to the strongly monotheistic biblical view. Bultmann opines, for example, that the affirmation "God is light and in him is no darkness at all" (I John 1:5) "probably contains polemic against Gnostic teachings which regarded the lower world of darkness as having originated by gradual emanations from the world of light."[7]

Now as Bultmann emphasizes, Gnosticism in the New Testament is dealt with not as an alien threat but as a phenomenon within the Church. (This was in fact a view taken by some others before Bultmann's time.) He argues most persuasively, however, that "Gnosticism probably penetrated into the Christian congregations through the medium of a Hellenistic Judaism that was itself in the grip of syncretism."[8] When Satan is called "the god of this world" (II Cor. 4:4), the "ruler of this world" (John 12:31; 14:30; 16:11), "the prince of the power of the air" (Ephesians 2:2) and the like, the New Testament authors are using Gnostic language.[9]

Gnosticism was, however, the sort of phenomenon that lent itself to an enormous variety of interpretations and was so inseparable from the religious modes of conceptualizing in the Mediterranean world that some of its forms were bound to seem (and indeed to be) dangerous to the apostles of the Christian Way who, while using the motifs consciously or otherwise, perceived the dangers that certain forms of Gnostic motifs posed to these apostles' proclamation of the Lordship of Christ. So they interlarded their proclamations with warnings, much as, when existentialist talk was at its height some decades ago, preachers who had been profoundly influenced by existentialist modes of thought would warn their hearers against certain nihilistic forms of existentialism. As some attentive but not very discriminating people among these present-day congregations have in fact come away with the general impression that existentialism is *per se* an evil that the Church must combat, so no doubt many in the early Church would have received a similar impression about Gnostic ideas, which they could no more possibly exclude from their thinking and outlook than we today could totally exclude from ours our own contemporary influences in music, art, literature, and philosophy, however much we might disapprove of some aspects of them.

No one could have faulted Gnosticism in the first-century Church because of its preoccupation with angels, for angels were firmly planted in the biblical canon. Nor could anyone have complained about the Gnostic preoccupation with demons, for the Gospels themselves (and no doubt oral and other traditions lying behind them) were full of accounts of demonic possession. Demons were very real to the peoples of the Mediterranean. The world was in the grip of the Evil One. Who else? Evil could not be attributed to the action of the One Holy God. The New Testament writers were not quarreling with the use of angels-and-demons language. What they feared was an inherited notion that the remedy against "the powers of darkness" might lie in knowledge of (as we might say) a spiritual chemistry. On the contrary, they proclaimed the remedy to be the power of Christ. Yet they recognized that there are indeed evil powers for Christ to vanquish. They affirmed only his infinite power to do so.

So much for the "powers of darkness"; but in Gnostic thought there are also the "powers of light": darkness is, in Gnostic dualism, the other side of light. These two fundamental categories in Gnostic thought appear throughout the New Testament, notably but by no means exclusively in John. Unless we see the thoroughly Gnostic thought-pattern of the New Testament writers we shall be misinterpreting them at almost every step. If we take away the Gnostic background we intolerably obscure the reason for their insistence on the supremacy of Christ, for his supremacy is meaningless except as a supremacy over that vast and superlatively important reality: the domain of these innumerable angelic powers, good and evil.

The war between Michael and his heavenly hosts, on the one hand, and Satan and his denizens, on the other, is not only real; it is infinitely more important than any other conflict we can imagine. Beside it all earthly wars are waged by mere puppets. Behind all earthly battles and struggles a war is being conducted among the angels, the spiritual powers, the outcome of which war is assured to us by the knowledge that Christ is Lord of all these awesomely real forces. Victory (a basic New Testament theme) is not victory over nothing; it is victory over the very real powers of darkness and the triumph of the powers of light. We cannot escape the fact that an understanding of the New Testament demands an understanding of the roots of the authors' thought in the Ancient Wisdom or Gnosis.

Gnosticism, which of course takes many forms, abounds in

reference to androgynous beings who are generally presented as superior to humanity as we know it. The androgyn, offspring of the original One and in some way a progenitor of the human race, is both male and female yet neither, since division into two sexes has not taken place. In some systems Sophia desired to have offspring apart from her male component and in doing so broke the perfection of the androgynous ideal. Yet even her offspring (Yaldabaoth, the Demiurge, an inferior God to whom was ascribed the creation of the material universe) was represented in some Gnostic systems as also androgynous.

The androgynous state is characteristically represented as superior to ours, so that the androgyn is a higher sort of being as is the angel in Judaeo-Christian tradition. The Gnostic exaltation of the androgyn reflects not only a longing for wholeness but also a disparagement of human sexuality as a fractured state. The Valentinian Gospel of Philip proclaims that when Eve was still in Adam death was unknown and that if he were to attain his former, original self, death would end. The notion of a superior, androgynous race of beings is a characteristic Gnostic theme, of which there are echoes in the words attributed by Mark to Jesus who, on being asked whose wife a woman would be after the resurrection, if on earth she had been married to seven husbands, affirmed that in heaven there is to be no more marrying, for we are to be "as the angels" (Mark 12:18–25). Of course the Sadducees who posed the question to Jesus were among those who, unlike the Pharisees, did not believe in resurrection (hence the implied mockery in their question); but no less plainly Jesus was chiding them for the crudity of their understanding of it. The resurrected state is represented as beyond sexuality as we know it. That fits the characteristic Gnostic hope of the re-establishment of an original or archetypal existence beyond, and superior to, human sexuality.

Whether we like it or not we must recognize that the androgynous ideal, so characteristic of Gnostic modes of thought, has secured a firm place (however disguised) in the mainstream of Christian thought and practice. The male-female polarity is recognized, of course, as inseparable from our human condition, so marriage is held in high esteem with sacramental status; but beyond and above it is a higher ideal still, symbolically represented in virginity and the celibate life. This exaltation of celibacy is no less obviously striking in the Greek Church than it is in the Roman, for although Greek priests may marry before ordination they may not do so afterwards (hence the popular simile "as precious as a Greek priest's wife") and no married priest may become a bishop, so that the episcopate is generally drawn from the monks, who of course are celibate.

What is the reason for the exaltation of celibacy? The common notion that it arises from some sort of "cultural homosexuality" in the Church is much too superficial to be adequate. It springs, rather, from an unconscious longing for the androgynous state in which the male-female polarity is unnecessary. The androgyn has a wholeness, an ontological integrity that in humans is fractured by the division into male and female. Because of this sexual polarity in us, male and female long for one another with a desire that is not only overwhelming but never permanently satiable. Whether we satisfy it or attempt to repress it, in the long run our longing is unsatisfied because our malaise springs not only from sexual apartness and loneliness, but also from an even deeper anguish: the longing for the integrity of the androgyn, in whom the fractured condition of our human sexuality is transcended by wholeness. Although the single life, with all its deprivation, cannot of course achieve that androgynous ideal, it *symbolizes* it and points the way to the higher mode of being.

Angels, whether conceived as enjoying a mode of existence that we have lost or as having one toward which we ought to be striving, represent the fulfilment of the androgynous ideal. They are neither male nor female, yet they are both. They are not hermaphroditic, yet neither are they sexless. Of course in art and literature all this is not easily expressed, but in one way or another the androgynous ideal is there. More will be said of this in Chapter 17.

Although the Hebrew prophets eloquently proclaimed monotheism, remnants of the old polytheistic ways of thinking are not difficult to find in popular Judaism of the later biblical period. As with saints later on in popular Catholicism, such polytheistic echoes found expression in beliefs about angels, who sometimes seem to be "adopted" into old polytheistic roles. One scholar, pointing to the popular beliefs about angels that Judaism would accommodate in later biblical times, writes as follows: "God's will in the world was executed by a multitude of such deputies. Not only is his revelation communicated through them, not only are they his instruments in providence and history, but the realm of nature is administered by them. The movements of the heavenly bodies are regulated by an angel who is appointed over all the luminaries of heaven. There are regents of the seasons, of months, and of days who ensure the regularity of the calendar; the sea is controlled by a mighty prince; rain and dew, frost and snow and hail, thunder and lightning, have their own presiding spirits."[10]

In medieval Jewish mystical literature, the earliest kabbalistic tradition is to be found in the Merkābah concept. The Merkābah or "Throne Chariot of God" provides a means of mystical procession through a series of heavenly halls, with angelic assistance. The Merkābah became the focal point of this tradition, which claims great antiquity. The literature contains long descriptions of how to make a safe transition through the heavenly halls. The aspirant must know, for instance, certain sacred passwords by means of which he can overcome demons he will encounter on his way. According to one of the most famous legends in this tradition, Enoch led such a holy life that God took him up to heaven and raised him to the first rank of angels, becoming an angel called Metatron, described as having flesh of fire, eyelashes of lightning, and eyes of flaming torches.

The Merkābah tradition, full of angelology, spawned other kabbalistic traditions in which angels played a central role. By the twelfth century C.E., for instance, a German kabbalistic school was in full flower and teaching a doctrine of the emanation from God of four "worlds." The scheme becomes extremely intricate and a description of it is far beyond the scope of a chapter such as this. Fundamentally, however, we find first of all a recognition that God is so far beyond us that all attempts to understand him are futile; nevertheless by mystical exercises one may come to know something of these "worlds." First (nearest to God) is a "world" in which God is united to his Shekhinah,[11] his feminine counterpart. The second world is formed from the lights that stream from the first "world." This second "world" is the abode of pure spirits, the highest ranking angels of the universe. These angels gather themselves round the Shekhinah to form her body. The third world is the abode of ten hosts of angels, who are specified by name. They are presided over by Metatron, who, as we have just seen, is identified with Enoch, translated into heaven. The fourth "world" is the world of human existence, the empirical or material world.

The notion of dimensions of being emanating from God and

becoming grosser as the emanations go farther and farther from their source is one that has counterparts in other Gnostic systems. Students of Plotinus and Erigena will recognize at once certain similarities in the systems of these thinkers. What is of special interest for our purpose, however, is that not only are angels a fundamental element in this kabbalistic structure; *a human being can be advanced to angelhood.* Enoch achieved such advancement, becoming even, in Metatron, Prince of the heavenly hosts. If Enoch could do all that, it must be open to any human being, if only one be holy enough, to attain angelic status. This is quite alien to both Jewish and Christian orthodoxy. The orthodox rabbis were generally very chary, to say the least, of angel-talk. The reason is easy to see. They feared that bringing angels too close to God was too reminiscent of the polytheism from which the ancient prophets had weaned the Hebrew people.

Gnostic systems, although they have much in common, take many forms. They tend to sprout very wild shoots and to create jungles of concepts that cry out for pruning by an Occam's razor. Nevertheless, they also contain the very stuff of religion. By cavalierly throwing them out, the institutional Church deprives itself of its own lifeblood. Paul, as a Hellenistic Jew, was well aware of both dangers and sought to distinguish the wheat from the chaff in gnostic systems, warning Timothy against "pseudo-gnosis" (I Timothy 6:20), while tirelessly teaching a Christian gnosis that implies and therefore includes *pistis,* faith.[12]

The history of Christian thought also includes, however, underground and vitally important traditions of mystical and theosophical concern having even deeper roots in the Ancient Wisdom or Gnosis, and hardly touching in any overt way the official doctrines and practices of the institutional Church. In that esoteric Christian spirituality the notion that we are attended by hosts of invisible helpers is so familiar as to be all but commonplace. Divine Being is seen to be regularly operating through the instrumentality of such "angels and ministers of grace" who have immense power both to protect us from evil forces and to advance our spiritual good. They are envisioned as beings more advanced than ourselves, yet not in a separate, higher state that we can never hope to attain. They may even be seen, in this kind of tradition, as somewhat like the *bodhisattvas* of Mahayana Buddhism: human beings who have attained a state qualifying them for "higher things" but who nevertheless, out of compassion and love for us, dally behind to give us their aid and to guide us onward. Since they may even be departed relatives and friends, the formal distinction made by the Church between angels and saints disappears in this Christian undercurrent.

Even, however, without recourse to what some may dub a byway in Christian tradition, one may well ask why the individual human being should be restricted to one guardian angel. Why not many such invisible helpers? The Bible itself suggests a bountiful supply of them. When Jesus had passed through the Great Temptation at the beginning of his ministry, angels, we are told, came and ministered to him. The notion of one guardian angel allotted to each individual, beautiful as it may be, may seem inadequate to those who have accustomed themselves to an awareness of a whole dimension of being in which such invisible helpers are constantly and copiously at work, each in a special way, not only by making mental suggestions to me but by prompting the thoughts and actions of others in such a way as is conducive to my protection from folly, and to prodding me to action I would be otherwise too timid or too irresolute to take.

With such an attitude, prayer will make much more sense to me, both petitionary (for myself) and intercessory (for others), since I will be less inclined to look for the direct answer that the spiritually immature expect. My prayers will foster in me instead a readiness to be on the *qui vive* for new strategies in God's campaign to help me without intruding upon the freedom that is both assured to me and imposed upon me by the divine act that creates me and forever lets me be. For I will never see these invisible helpers as cajoling me, let alone coercing me, into actions against my will. I will see their strategy as much more delicate and subtle. They know the terrain of the invisible, spiritual dimension far better than I, and are much more skilled at coping with its agencies.

Biblical support for thinking in terms of vast multitudes of heavenly helpers is plentiful. The Psalmist tells me that though ten thousand fall by my side, Yahweh will put me "in his angels' charge" to guard me wherever I go (Ps. 91:7–13). The writer to the Hebrews assures me that I am on my way to a heavenly Jerusalem in which millions[13] of angels have gathered with the whole Church in which everyone is a first-born son and a citizen of heaven (Hebrews 12:22 ff. Jerusalem Bible). Paul, relying on rabbinic tradition as he so often does, tells the Galatians that the Torah itself was promulgated by angels, with Moses as but a spokesman (Galatians 3:19). According to Luke, Jesus himself assures me that if I declare myself for him in the presence of men he will declare himself for me in the presence of God's angels (Luke 12:8 ff.). According to much biblical testimony, such angelic aid as I may expect is to come to me from a plurality of these agents of divine Being. When, however, we read that "the angel of Yahweh" appeared, we are to understand that Yahweh's presence was manifested. The angel is not merely an envoy plenipotentiary; he *is* the divine presence.

5

SATAN: THE REALM OF ANGELS GONE WRONG

The seventy-two came back rejoicing. "Lord," they said, "even the devils submit to us when we use your name." He [Jesus] said to them, "I watched Satan fall like lightning from heaven."

LUKE 10:17 F.

uman imagination is more easily stirred by Satan than by God. That is because evil sounds more sinister, more devious, more intriguing, and therefore more interesting than goodness. Mystery and murder, adultery and fraud: these are the very stuff of the novels and films that captivate people's fancy and entertain them in an idle hour. Hagiography may edify, but it is inherently dull. So sex and violence, whether elegantly decorated and served on a silver platter to trained minds and sophisticated literary palates, or dished out crude and brassy to hordes of passive television-watchers, are the main ingredients to be stirred into any script that has entertainment as its goal.

In the Middle Ages (and indeed much later) the novel as we know it was not yet born. Morality plays and other forms of drama and literature provided, however, satisfaction of the human appetite for watching evil as a spectator sport. The focus was on the Devil and his hellish hosts, who in the popular imagination were ever on the prowl. Here popular imagination had the full support of the Church, which took Satan and his legions very seriously indeed and whose theologians discussed the subject in their own learned way and in considerable detail. They had plenty of pabulum to work

44

from, for as we have seen the tradition was an ancient one going back to New Testament times and stretching much farther back into the mists of antiquity in the most primitive forms of religion.

The Church, moreover, could claim the fullest biblical authority for its preoccupation with the Devil. In the New Testament there are not only abundant references to him, as we have seen, but a special warning (I Peter 5:8) that came to be regularly intoned in Compline, sung just before retiring to sleep: "Be sober, be vigilant; because your adversary the devil, as a roaring lion, walketh about, seeking whom he may devour."

Satan played a fundamental role in the Church's teaching. The Fourth Lateran Council (1215) declared it is a matter of faith to be accepted by all Christians that Satan and the other devils are by nature spirits created by God and therefore originally good, and that they "fell into sin of their own free will," so being "eternally damned." The Fathers of this general council affirmed that it was at the instigation of Satan that Adam sinned. The Council of Trent (1549–1560) specified that the human race consequently passed into the power of the Devil. Such indeed was the ideological background, comprising as it did the notion of an ideal state of both angels and men and their subsequent fall from that state. Apart from that scenario the notion of salvation through Christ and indeed the Person and Work of Christ would have seemed meaningless and therefore unintelligible.

From the well-established belief in the fall of the rebellious angels and their interest in seducing humanity to their evil purposes, two very important consequences ensued. First, in popular piety and outlook devils fired imaginations in such a way as to strike terror and yet provide scope for dramatic amusement. Second, the learned had much difficulty in trying to deal with the impossible theological and philosophical difficulties attending the traditional account of how such lofty beings as angels could fall from their noble estate, and how such innocent creatures as Adam and Eve could be seduced by the Devil and so bring such disastrous consequences to the entire human race.

Let us look first at the second of these two points. It was generally recognized by the Church that the angels are impeccable, that is, such is their state of perfection that they cannot stand in any danger of sinning as men and women do. How then, did Lucifer and his rebellious cohorts sin and therefore fall so low? Thomas Aquinas addressed himself to such problems about the angels with his characteristic acuity. He recognized two opinions on the time of the fall of the angels: some held that it was immediately after their creation; others opined that there was an interval. Thomas, preferring the former of these two views, held that Lucifer, like all the angels, was created in a state of grace yet instantly exercised in a wrong direction the free will with which all angels are endowed. Otherwise he could not have sinned, since angels, Thomas affirmed, achieve everlasting bliss the instant they do one meritorious act and thereafter they are so close to God that it is impossible for them to turn away from him. Hence the other angels (those who did not rebel) can never sin. He allowed, however, that one *might* hold that the angels were not created in a state of grace, in which case there could have been an interval between Lucifer's creation and his fall. In either case, however, an angel becomes impeccable once he has freely chosen to do one good act and raises no barrier against his being confirmed in grace.[1]

One can see how vexing was the problem and how baffling the solution, even for so ingenious a schoolman as Thomas. Neither Luther nor Calvin depart very substantially from the medieval scholastic tradition and teaching in respect to the fall of the angels. Their fall was different from the fall of humans, which was attributed to Satan's evil and destructive intervention. The presuppositions behind all these teachings were such as to breed an endless host of insoluble problems.

The Devil, however, was so deeply entrenched in Christian lore from the earliest times that belief in his reality was assured whatever the theologians were or were not able to do about explaining how he came about, and how he and his cohorts could have so sinned when it was inconceivable that good angels like Michael and Gabriel could sin. This brings us back to the first point: the Devil in popular imagination.

Satan and his legions were active everywhere and at all times in the medieval imagination. The Devil was extremely cunning and able to disguise himself in a vast variety of forms. Although in fact hideous in every way, with horns, cloven feet, a face on his backside, a tail, and a body all hairy and horrible, and leaving behind him an unspeakably loathsome stench, he could (and often did) disguise himself as an angel of light. He could also engage in other metamorphoses such as changing himself into a seductively beautiful young girl in order to tempt a monk, or into a handsome young man in order to seduce servant girls or others. If successful, he would then change back into his standard appearance and leeringly carry his victim off howling and screaming to hell. He was often behind village disputes, which he loved to foster. In short, he was behind all evils that befell anyone and all troubles that beset society. He delighted in parodying the holiest mysteries of the Faith. He had innumerable aides and offspring, for although sexless he could assume a human form and impregnate unfortunate women, which was of course in flagrant opposition to the "official" view of the theologians, according to which he is a spirit and sexless. In folklore his relation to his aids and progeny is often obscure: monsters, werewolves, vampires, witches, demons, imps are among the denizens of his domain. What is always clear is that he is the Prince of Hell and the Enemy of God. The word "Satan" means "adversary" or "enemy."

The Devil was treated extensively in vernacular literature and since the writers were less tied to doctrine than were the theologians, they often introduced interesting modifications of the "official" view. For example, the Devil could be portrayed as a vassal who betrayed the trust of his *seigneur* or lord. Such imagery, in a feudal society, could be readily understood by all. Simple people could see wherein the Devil's wrong lay: he had violated his lord's trust and in doing so had upset the right order of things. At the same time the imagery could arouse a certain admiration for the Devil's daring. It was somewhat as in a modern film about, say, a million-dollar bank robbery: we see that such an act is fundamentally against the interest of our society and must not be tolerated. We deplore the robber's lawlessness and applaud his capture and punishment; yet in the excitement of the drama we cannot help admiring his audacity, which is so far beyond ours. So fear of the Devil could be tempered by a secret and sometimes delicious envy of his prowess and admiration for his cunning.

In art we have something similar. In early medieval art the Devil is often depicted with wings much like those of the good angels. From about the twelfth century he tends to be equipped with bat-like wings. Although usually black, he could also be pale gray, symbolic of disease and death, or purple, suggestive of the dark, foggy air contrasted with the glowing brightness of the good angels. In later medieval art he could be red, the color of hell's fire, but that was a departure from the older tradition favoring black. Other features could be introduced at the artist's whim: spindly legs, distended abdomen, and unkempt hair could all serve to make him at once frightening and revolting. He could serve not only as the enemy to be feared but as the scapegoat on which to put the blame for all ills: the whipping boy, if you will. There are even stories of medieval saints who, having been troubled by visitations from the Devil, resorted to whipping him literally. One may ask, how could they do so? The answer is that (a) the popular imagination in the Middle Ages and later could easily be fired to the point of seeing a realistic vision of the Devil as iconographically represented in art and that (b) devout monks and nuns were accustomed to the use of a "discipline" or whip as an instrument of penance. To use such a whip on a vision of the Devil might well seem a spontaneous as well as a correct reaction to such an appearance of the Enemy. Often, however, it was the Devil who seized his victims and thrashed them with infernal whips or rods. The Devil could be pathetic or fearsome, repulsive or alluring, bloated or skinny, leering or sour. The torments he could inflict were as varied as his guises, ranging (as in Dante's *Inferno*) from fiery furnaces to frozen lakes, from the comparatively mild punishment of the wanton who are everlastingly swirled by fierce winds to the tortures of Judas whom Satan personally chomps incessantly in his gnawing mouth.

Despite the multiplicity of forms the Devil can assume, his role *par excellence* (so far as humankind is concerned) is that of tempter. The significance of this role is important, for although God gives Satan much rope, human beings are still free to choose between what they know to be right and what they know to be wrong. They need not heed the Devil's tempting voice and the less they heed it the purer will be their vision and thus the more clearly will they discern the Devil's cunning. So however wantonly the medieval artist might depict man as at the mercy of the Devil's wiles, the theologians left no doubt that he could not be solely to blame for human sins, because all he can do is to tempt man. Man can resist him. Goethe, in *Faust,* recaptures this ancient theme. Mephistopheles (Satan) makes a bet with God: he claims he can lead Faust to hell if only God will let him try. God grants his permission, but under the condition that Faust's freedom of choice remain inviolate. In other words, Satan is to be allowed to tempt Faust but not to coerce him: a fair bargain according to the traditional rules. We can see, then, why "The Devil made me do it" is a laughable line.

What are the instruments used by Satan and his minions in his role as tempter? Of course devils are pragmatists. They will use whatever weapons work best. Nevertheless, two are specified in the traditional baptismal ceremony. The candidate or his sponsor is called upon to renounce the world, the flesh, and the Devil, in that order. That means, in effect, that one first recognizes the Devil's two favorite weapons and the works he achieves by means of them and renounces these works before renouncing the Devil himself. By "the world" is meant the lure of money and power, the desire for which is the root of evil *(radix malorum)* for it is an expression in our societal framework of the more fundamental pride that at a higher level was responsible for Satan's own downfall. (As we shall see much later in looking at Eve through Milton's eyes, she, too, was seduced not by sexual temptation, as is vulgarly supposed, but by the titillation of her vanity.) After the world, then, the next obstacle to salvation is the flesh. Satan especially delights in the use of this weapon since, being pure spirit, he is immune to its temptations, despite popular superstition to the contrary. From his detached position he can exploit human susceptibility to this temptation as deftly as an unscrupulous scoundrel with all his wits about him can rob a drunk. (The general theory seems to be that although Satan can appear in lascivious guises to molest women, his aim is not to gratify his own raging lust, which he merely assumes, since he, being spirit, is unencumbered by such desires, but to enslave her to the flesh and so weaken her spiritual vitality to the point where he can drag her off to perdition.) Finally, the baptismal candidate renounces Satan himself.

Although baptismal rites have varied, most of them (at least in the West) have prominently included actual exorcism of the Devil— that is, a priestly command to the Devil, in the name of Christ, to depart and let the peace of God reside unimpeded in the soul of the baptismal candidate.[2] What comes through over and over again is the notion that humanity in its unregenerate state is not just enfeebled (for example by the frailty of the flesh or even by personal vanity or power-mania) but is actually in bondage to the Devil. The baptismal candidate must therefore be released from the prison in which Satan holds him or her.[3] This release does not insure that the Devil will not return to tempt and torment the soul even after the regenerating effects of baptism, but it does accomplish something far more important: it removes the primary obstacle to salvation: the bondage to Satan which, if not removed, would have kept the soul perpetually in his grip.

We should note in passing here that most of the great religions of the world have a figure who corresponds in one way or another to Satan. In Buddhism, for example, Māra may be taken as a counterpart. True, fundamental differences in the philosophical presuppositions of Christianity and Buddhism produce some differences. For instance, while Satan is generally seen by Christians as the great deceiver, "the Father of lies," Buddhist writers allude rather to his capacity for confusing and perplexing people. Broadly speaking, one might perhaps say that Satan functions primarily by undermining the wills of men and women, while Māra obscures their perception of truth. On the whole, however, such differences seem comparatively superficial. Both religions see the Evil One as dark. Both talk of bondage or fetters. Buddhism does seem to invest Māra with a splendor and majesty not generally associated with Satan and emphasizes the shiny attractiveness of evil in a way not typical of Christian language; yet Christian documents do not by any means exclude the perception of evil as glittering tinsel and of course Satan's other name is Lucifer, the Bearer of Light.[4]

In Islam, Iblis (or Shaytan as he is sometimes called) is more clearly the counterpart of Satan, whom God allows to roam the world and to tempt man although, as in Christian teaching, preserving man's freedom of choice. The Muslim account of the fall of Iblis parallels the Christian one, with one exception: the notion that any creature, even the highest of the angels, should dare to envy Allah has generally seemed intolerable to Islamic thought, so Muslims hold that it was envy of humanity that caused Satan's fall. The reason he declined to obey Allah's command to bow before man was that he envied man. His fall was due, not to an arrogant pride that made him want to be God but, rather, to envy at God's later and superior creation: man. This view, although aberrant from the mainstream of Christian teaching, has not been entirely without its advocates in Christianity. No less a churchman than the second-century Irenaeus, for instance, espoused a somewhat similar position. So despite certain technical, theological differences, Satan and Iblis function very much the same way in relation to humans.

The tradition of demonic possession goes back, as we all know, to the New Testament, where any form of psychosis is described in terms of the patient's "having a devil." This notion of a person's body being taken over by a demon is ancient and persists in some circles today. Whatever one may think of it, one should notice that it does not necessarily imply any direct alignment with Satan. Demons who inhabit bodies seem to be much less audacious than is the Devil's wont. They look for shelter in an available body as vermin slink into whatever hole they can find for protection and warmth. So despite the harm they do to body and mind they seem to lack the superlative malice of the fallen angels for whom such attitudes and behavior would be beneath their dignity. Not all the denizens of hell qualify for inclusion in a study of angels. The Devil and his cohorts might use other infernal powers such as demons and imps to serve them, as a vicious empire-builder might wage bacteriological warfare against his enemies; but such bacteria would be far indeed from being commissioned officers in his army.

Does the Devil exist? Of course as he stands in either theology or folklore his name is a metaphor, as indeed is every term we use about the cosmos. The question is, rather, what is its metaphorical function? He stands for evil, but for more than evil in general, which is a vague and confusing concept since it must include all sorts of evils that are traditionally called "natural," such as earthquakes and floods, in contradistinction to the "moral" evils we humans bring about in such wanton profusion in every society. Whatever kind of evil Satan symbolizes, it is not the former kind which, after all, is only an evil to us if we happen to be in the middle of it, nor yet is it even the "moral" kind that is the result of human waywardness and folly. No, whatever it is, it is an evil that we see beyond all these: a warping of the order that we see in the universe and when we talk of a cosmos (which etymologically *means* "order"), a power at work that is beyond our control, for which we cannot individually or communally take the blame, even though we may be its pawns. For instance, despite all the strength of the case for pacifism and outlawing war, our century has been plagued with global conflicts that have caused unspeakable misery and have done much to wreck great civilizations. Yet their occurrence, though human greed and other vices play a part in it, does not seem to be wholly explicable in human terms. War is indeed more like a virus attacking humanity. Disease also, in spite of the stupendous progress in medicine in the past fifty years or so, seems beyond human control. No sooner have we found a cure for one disease than another, hitherto unknown, rears its head. In exasperation at our human impotence in face of these seemingly insurmountable problems we talk (metaphorically, of course) of the diabolical or demonic character of the forces that so plague humankind. Are we then merely venting the perplexity and bewilderment that we all feel about such evils by oblique allusions in archaic language? (" 'Evil' is too pallid a word—it's positively 'diabolical'!") Or is it perhaps that if we are to take angels seriously we may have to take no less seriously their demonic counterparts: the "angels gone wrong"?

6

LOVE AFFAIRS BETWEEN WOMEN AND
FALLEN ANGELS

When men had begun to be plentiful on the earth, and daughters
had been born to them, the sons of God, looking at the daughters of
men, saw they were pleasing, so they married as many as they
chose. . . . The Nephilim were on earth at that time (and even
afterward) when the sons of God resorted to the daughters of men,
and had children by them. These are the heroes of days gone by,
the famous men.

GENESIS 6:1–4 (JERUSALEM BIBLE)

One of the strangest allusions in
the entire Bible is to be found in the passage (Genesis 6:1–4) in
which we read of the sexual union of angels with mortal women.
Of course the notion that the gods occasionally desire and seduce
mortal girls is familiar to all students of classical Greek mythology.
The legend of Leda and the Swan is but one example. Leda was the
daughter of Thestios, King of Aetolia, and the wife of Tyndareus,
King of Sparta. The great Zeus, no less, father of the gods, who
presided over the entire pantheon, desired her. With a skillful use
of his divine power he transformed himself into a swan, the better
to seduce her with his beauty and grandeur. The ruse worked.
Under the guise of a swan he proved irresistible to Leda, the lady
of his desire. The children of this remarkable union were the
Dioscuri, half mortal, half immortal. These hybrid offspring were
predictably suprahuman yet not quite gods. They were intermediate
between deities and humans. They were supposed to appear in the
kind of electrical phenomenon that eventually came to be called St.
Elmo's fire.

53

Such cavortings in pagan mythology astonish nobody. They are the sort of stuff out of which the great ancient mythologies are made. To find such a story in the Bible, however, does tend to surprise, not to say jolt, even the most casual reader. It does not seem to fit the biblical scenario. As a matter of fact, when the second edition of the Bishops' Bible (published in England in 1572) appeared, adorned with pagan illustrations that included one depicting the legend of Leda and the Swan, it not only shocked the Puritan party in the English Church but offended most people, for they instinctively felt such adornment to be alien to the spirit of the Bible.

Yet, although their instinct was no doubt right in principle, the notion is in fact part of the very complex literature we call the Bible. It was part of the heritage of those who wrote it. According to the passage in Genesis just quoted, it was after humanity had been well established on the earth that the "sons of God" took notice of the fairness of the daughters of men and desired them. Their progeny were the Nephilim: the giant heroes of old. The Hebrew word used here for God is the plural *Elohim* and there can be little if any doubt that the story, probably introduced by way of prelude to the account of the Flood, has been borrowed by the writer from an ancient myth that has counterparts in many other primitive cultures in antiquity. The Titans in Greek mythology have some functional resemblance to the Nephilim. The Genesis passage is echoed in later books, canonical and otherwise, e.g., Jude v v. 6–7 and Ecclesiasticus (Sirach) 16:7: "God did not pardon the giants of old." There is some ambiguity about the nature of the progeny of angels and humans: sometimes they are giants, heroes, supermen; sometimes they are demons. The early Christian writers who allude to such unions seem to incline to the latter opinion. Justin Martyr, for instance, expresses such a view in his *Apologia* and Tertullian calls them deserters of God and lovers of women *(desertores Dei, amatores feminarum)*. Only after some centuries does the idea recede, being relegated from faith to fable. Demons were still taken seriously in the medieval world, as we have seen, but they were considered by theologians to be evil *spirits*. They are enormously powerful, but the notion of their having a divine-human ancestry had been discarded.

Nevertheless, as we have just seen in the last chapter, the concept lingered on in odd ways, for example, in the bizarre notion that the Devil and his cohorts could *assume* the body of a human male and seduce women or (as the case required) assume the body of a beautiful young girl and seduce a holy monk. Everyone could see, of course, that such trickery was in every way despicable, but what else could one expect of a devil? Besides, the Devil is at war with God and in warfare one does not stop to consider ethical niceties.

The interest for us lies in the fact that in one way or another the corporeality of angels was preserved in folklore, whatever the theologians might say. Moreover, although angels were above the divided state in which we humans are as "mere" men or "mere" women, when they "went wrong" they could and did fall into human sexuality in the worst possible way. Here one must remember that the medieval people, generally speaking, had a very earthy view of sex, which they did not invest with the redeeming, romantic dimensions it has today among civilized people. It symbolized the bestial. The androgynous ideal, on the other hand, implied embodiment without the brokenness of masculinity and femininity. The angel who fell could very easily assume a body equipped with the dividedness of a fallen state, that is, with sexual organs, male or female.

Not only did the concept of angelic embodiment linger on in folklore. It also eventually affected, if it did not determine, the mould of some mainstream religious ideas about angels. What will become particularly significant for us as our study develops is the notion, primitive as its origins may have been, that angels and humans can possibly consort together in such a way as to have progeny. For this means that, contrary to our customary presuppositions about angels, they are represented as closer to human beings than we would suppose.

By the time of Jesus they are clearly perceived as being above sexual union, as is implicit in his answer (Mark 12:25) to the Sadducees' tricky question. Yet although they are "spirits whose work is service, sent to help those who will be the heirs of salvation" (Hebrews 1:14), they are not incorporeal, not disembodied spirits. No, that they have an embodiment of some kind (a "glorious" body) is clearly implied by Jesus when he states that men and women, *after the resurrection,* are to be *like the angels.* Closely though they company with God, they do have an affinity with us, having an embodiment such as Paul promises those of us who attain to resurrection, that is, not in our present physical body but in a more glorious, more luminous one. In this they are more like us than like God who is pure spirit (John 4:24). The glorious appearance ascribed to the angels in passages such as Daniel 10:6 seems to be comparable to that of Christ's Transfiguration and to that state in which he is portrayed in the Apocalypse (Revelation 1:14–16).

Even such a transfigured embodiment implies finitude, limitation, creatureliness and therefore some sort of affinity with human beings. It also implies the capacity for temptation.[1] That is why they are capable of having "left their first estate" *(tēn heautōn archēn)* as some of them did, becoming "angels of the Devil" (Matthew 25:41; Revelation 12:7, 9). Even late in the Quattrocento we still find vestiges of the ancient notion of fallen angels impelled by diabolical lust to rape their victims. So we can see in a detail of the *Inferno* by Luca Signorelli, dating back to about the year 1500, in the Cappella di San Brizio in the Cathedral of Orvieto, a woman being carried off on a devil's back, her hands pinioned over his ugly wings and held secure in his, while he leers lasciviously at his conquest. When angels fall, their rarefied and translucent bodies degenerate into bodies lacking even the lustre of human beings and their passions are as bestial as their intent is diabolical. We humans, being (as Pascal put it) "half beasts, half angels," have an affinity with both. We hover between the bestial and the angelic.

So the ancient myths about the love affairs of some of the "sons of Elohim" persist in human consciousness. They are the suprahuman beings, the glorious ones, who stand as intermediaries between God and humanity, exalted above our present state as human begins, yet capable of a more extreme warping than that of which we in our humbler state are capable. Yet the offspring of their fornication with mortal women reflect something of their parents' original sublime grandeur, as well as the ruthless amorality that we associate with great conquerors and dictators. In the Napoleons of this world remains, however corrupted, a residue of suprahuman grandeur.

The angels, then, in fable and in faith, hover near to us and we oscillate between the good ones and the bad. Such is the mythological model we have inherited. It has served well and still serves well to symbolize the precariousness of our human condition, poised as we are on a tightrope with heaven above and hell below. So we depict the frailty of man, but the angels, whatever we may suppose them to be, are no less susceptible than we to moral danger. Indeed their capacity for falling is commensurate with the greater glory and grandeur of their state. That is why the good angels are ideal helpers for us. They are at a level at which they are not tempted by the trivialities that tempt us, yet they know well, at a higher level than ours, what temptation is and how terrible are its consequences. This is the great mythological truth about angels and ourselves that has persisted through all the vicissitudes of Christian thought and all the developments of mainstream Christian theology. The Bible is saturated with it, although, except for that remarkable passage in Genesis where it is blatantly, not to say crudely, enunciated, allusions to it are generally discreet and decently clad in the garb of more developed and delicate symbolism.

In Christian practice a strong tradition prevails concerning the "testing" of spirits. It goes back to the New Testament itself. "It is not every spirit, my dear people," writes the author of the First Letter of John (I John 4:1) "that you can trust; test them, to see if they come from God." He goes on (I John 4:6): "But we are the children of God, and those who know God listen to us; those who are not of God refuse to listen to us. This is how we can tell the spirit of truth from the spirit of falsehood." Tests for discerning good spirits from evil ones have been developed by the great masters of Christian spirituality such as Teresa and John of the Cross. In Christian spirituality the fundamental principle behind all such tests, however, is that proclaimed by the writer of the Fourth Gospel: the sheep know their shepherd and recognize him as he recognizes them. Moreover, there are other sheep "not of this fold" who will recognize him as their shepherd when they hear his voice, "and there will be one flock and one shepherd" (John 10:14–16). He whose heart is pure will recognize pure love when he sees it. He will not be deceived by frauds. So even when Satan and his minions present themselves deceitfully in alluring guises, as is their wont, in dreams and visions, they can succeed in their evil ploys only to the extent that their victims have already so strayed as to have lost that purity of heart that confers the salutary discernment of good from evil spirits. The most terrible of the afflictions that attend him who loses purity of heart is that he loses with it the power to detect evil intent when it approches him as a wolf attired in the benign clothing of a sheep. He is an easy prey: a sitting duck for the Devil. He has lost the clarity of moral vision that penetrates every disguise and sees through to the spiritual reality behind it.

In the ancient fables about gods and angels who go whoring after the "daughters of men," we have a paradigm of moral degeneration. It serves as a sort of archetype of bestiality in the sexual life of a human being: the ultimate corruption. (We have already noted the general absence of the romantic element in the medieval outlook on sexuality.) But it also draws to our attention the notion that if indeed there is a realm of angelic beings, such beings, for all the grandeur of their embodiment are nevertheless in some sense our kin: creatures like ourselves standing together in loving awe before God our Creator. That very Jewish insight is an inheritance that has been well preserved and vivaciously developed in Christian thought and practice.

12. PUTTI FROM POMPEII.
Casa dei Vettii, Pompeii.

13. GIRL ANGEL.
Niccolo dell Arca
(15th century),
Kneeling Angel. Arca
di San Domenico,
Bologna.

14. BOY ANGEL.
   Michelangelo Buonarroti (1475–1564), *Kneeling Angel*. Arca di San
   Domenico. Bologna.

15. LADY ANGELS.
    Wilton Dyptich (ca. 1377–1413). Gothic. National Gallery, London.

16. TINY TOT ON GUARD.
J. H. Ketten, *Emblem-boek*. Amsterdam,
1699.

17. TEENAGE ANGEL.
Gianlorenzo Bernini
(1598–1680),
Santa Teresa.
Santa Maria della
Vittoria, Rome.

18. SOME ANGELS HAVE SWORDS.
Albrecht Dürer (1471–1528), *Apokalypsis.*

19. JACOB'S ANGELS.
H. van Rijn Rem-
brandt (1600–1669),
The Dream of Jacob.
Pen and ink drawing.
Rijksmuseum, Am-
sterdam.

20. SOUND THE TRUMPET!
Trumpeting angel.
Romanesque. Strasbourg
Cathedral, France.

21. MADONNA AND HER
HEAVENLY COURT (right).
Cimabue (1272–1302),
Madonna with Angels.
Uffizi, Florence.

22. ANGELS ADORING MADONNA.
   Giotto di Bondone (1266–1337), *Madonna with Angels*. Uffizi,
Florence.

7

THE DEVELOPMENT OF OUR AWARENESS OF INVISIBLE HELPERS

... it becomes a probability of the highest order that there are or have been or will be beings that surpass man in the hierarchy of beings.

JOHN MACQUARRIE, *Principles of Christian Theology*

$\mathcal{S}$piritually discerning people of all ages including our own have always been in one way or another distinctly aware of the action and influence of "invisible helpers": beings who, whatever we may choose to call them, are our superiors in spiritual attainment. The notion is very familiar, of course, in modern spiritualistic literature and practice, but it is fundamental to the religious consciousness at all stages of development. Indeed, spirituality may be said to consist in large measure of such awareness of activity around us in a higher dimension of being.

Critique of such an interpretation may come from a wide spectrum of standpoints. Freudians may feel satisfied in interpreting such awareness in terms of the "super-ego" in the human psyche itself. At the other end of the interpretative spectrum, some (for example many conservative Protestants) will ask: "Why angels? Is not God always ready to help? And is not the Risen Christ the only Mediator in transactions between God and man?"

To the first of these objections the reply may be made as follows. Of course mental awareness of everything must occur "somewhere within" the mind of man; but the notion that it has its source there alone is like a child's belief that what he sees on the screen of the television set in his room originates in that box. It is to confuse the receiver with the transmitting station.

To the second objection one may point out that the awareness, although it is awareness of the presence and action of the Eternal One, is an awareness of specific concern and assistance from beings who, however superior to us, are nevertheless finite beings who seem to be charged with a specific mission. So it is as if, when I tell you of my experience of rain or snow or sunshine, you were to contradict me, saying that what I experienced was none of these but nature itself. Of course it was nature, but nature manifesting itself in a specific form. When the ground is parched after a long drought it does not cry out for nature; it cries out for rain. After a long northern winter it likewise cries out, not for nature, but for sunshine.

The symbolism to express this awareness will vary. Symbols always do, since they must conform to the psychological structure to which they are adapted. The invisible "ministers of grace" may be construed as more or less independent gods and goddesses as they are in polytheistic societies. Or again they may conform to a monotheistic structure, in which case they will be strictly emissaries of the One, Sovereign God. Certain imagery, however, does tend to be very widespread. For example, the experience is one of a presence that in some way *hovers* over or around the person experiencing it; hence the appropriateness of the wings, although modern technology might today provide other, perhaps better, symbols of angelic presence.

What I see in the notion of angelic presence is the expression of a profoundly important reality of the religious consciousness: that while I am left alone to work out my problems according to the freedom allotted to me within a wide range of circumstance, I am not left entirely alone to make any fatal error into which my frailty and weakness might lead me. Not only do certain suggestions come to me unexpectedly; I perceive events, sometimes long after they have occurred, that seem in peculiarly apposite ways to have ministered to my well-being or to have prevented my falling into a trap. It may even be as if a particular danger for me had been foreseen, arising out of the wide freedom I enjoy, and that a specific strategy had been developed to save me from it without interfering with my freedom, which has remained inviolate throughout, as indeed it must if I am to make any spiritual progress.

If there are such good, protective agencies, are there also evil ones, as much religious tradition would suggest? While the concept of a personal devil may seem to many a barbarous archaism, at least some of the evil that emerges in human relations and events does seem peculairly demonic in character. That some evil agency stalks us for prey or, in the picturesque language of the Bible, that our "enemy the Devil prowls around like a roaring lion, looking for someone to eat" (I Peter 5:8), hardly seems so weird or archaic as it might have seemed to those who lived before Belsen and Buchenwald and other twentieth-century horrors.

What principally distinguishes the religious consciousness, however, is an awareness of invisible helpers, superior intelligences, that are working under the benevolent captaincy of the Eternal One. In no way does this diminish the importance or significance that Christians see in the unique mediatorship of Christ, who not only is to be attended by angels when he comes in glory but humbly received their ministrations during his earthly life. Who or what are they, these ministrants and attendants of divine Being?

If we are to accept, as surely we must, an evolutionary understanding of the entire creative process, we cannot talk as did our forefathers of the creation of one species after another, as though cattle would be created on one day, men another, and angels on yet a different occasion. We must think, rather, of an eternal process of creativity in which we must expect always to be standing between stages of being less advanced than ourselves and other stages more advanced. In the inconceivably vast reaches of the universe, insofar as we know it, there is plenty of room for beings superior to us, both in intelligence and in other ways, who might well behave toward us under the direction of God in the manner ascribed to them in the Bible and celebrated in Christian tradition. At any rate, surely anyone who is in any way inclined to see creative divine Being at the heart of all things will be at least open to the possibility that angels appositely symbolize manifestations of God's presence. Those others who are not disposed to such methods of conceptualization or are unaccustomed to them may nevertheless entertain as reasonable the notion of the existence of a stage of evolutionary development higher than our own, such as the one angels have traditionally represented.

If, contrary to the medieval schoolmen's view of angels, we envision them as representing higher stages than our own in the evolution of the hierarchy of created beings, they need no longer seem mere creatures of religious fancy. They may become at least plausible. Professor John Macquarrie of Oxford recognizes this, although for one reason or another he has seemed reluctant to work out its full implications.[1] He acknowledges, however, that "as we learn more and more of the inconceivable vastness of space and time and of the infinite proliferation of worlds, it becomes a probability of the highest order that there are or have been or will be beings that surpass man in the hierarchy of beings,"[2] although man does seem to stand "at the apex of that hierarchy of beings that can be observed on our planet."[3]

No matter how we try to conceive of beings superior to ourselves (on other planets, for example), we must recognize that, to the extent that they are superior to us, we cannot really hope to understand them. Not only cannot a mouse hope to understand a man; a less advanced type of human being cannot be expected to understand the workings of the mind of a highly developed one, to say nothing of that of a Leonardo or a Goethe. Nevertheless, since our state of consciousness is such that we can distinguish levels of consciousness and evolutionary development less advanced than our own, the concept of levels of consciousness and evolutionary development higher than our own need not be entirely beyond us. We all have the capacity to perceive, however meagerly, wherein we are defective and therefore what it might be like to enjoy a state of existence not subject to such defects. To take a pedestrian example, we can easily see how a person of very limited musical ability and training can appreciate and admire the virtuosity of a musical genius although remaining quite unable to emulate it. What athlete does not wish he could have even better prowess than he does have? What orator does not wish he could be more persuasive still? At least one knows what it would *mean* to be able to move with the speed of light and grasp a highly complex problem in the flicker of an eyelid. So conceiving beings superior to ourselves is not entirely beyond our capacity.

If I can conceive of beings of greater mental agility than the greatest human genius and of greater co-ordination in the use of whatever kind of embodiment they may have, surely I can also conceive of them as having a higher moral development and as exhibiting a richer, more disinterested, and more effective love than even the noblest of human beings. Moreover, if I reflect on the tragedy of a great mind that has lost its grip or gone to seed, I can understand very well how terrible would be the tragedy of the fall of such a superior being. All our treasures, moral or mental, are carried precariously. There is no absolute assurance that a man or woman of seemingly noble ideals will not become soured and cynical a few years hence and turn into a hideous caricature of what he or she once was, becoming for us a fallen idol. "The man who thinks he is safe must be careful that he does not fall," writes Paul to the Corinthians (I Corinthians 10:12). The higher one's attainment, the greater the fall. The concept of fallen angels is not, then, so absurd as some contemporary theologians have supposed. While no one today would interpret neuroses and psychoses as necessarily resulting from the direct action of demonic agencies (as the New Testament writers, following the practice of their day, commonly do), the possibility that evil agencies as well as good ones exist in dimensions of being beyond us is not to be summarily excluded. Nor should the recognition of such a possibility unduly frighten us. So long as our faith in God remains lively and constant we may rest assured of having the protection of those superior beings, those invisible helpers, those ministers of grace, who are better geared to God's purposes and more effective than we can be in working them out.

The concept of superior beings such as angels has at any rate one extremely important value. It frees us from the parochialism of seeing Planet Earth as the focus of all creation and humanity as the end of the process of evolution. As we look back many millions of years ago into our humble beginnings in the evolutionary process and perceive also the gigantic developments in the human race itself, from its lowest to its highest exemplars, we shall be indeed ludicrously unimaginative if we do not also look, at least in some measure, beyond our human condition. Those who, like Nietzsche and Ibsen and Shaw, could talk of the "Ubermensch"or "superman" perceived the fundamental implications of an evolutionary understanding of the universe at a time when less was known of its staggering magnitude than is known today. The writers of the New Testament knew little even of the magnitude of Planet Earth (and nothing at all, of course, of the Americas) and were accordingly very limited in their capacity to envision the astronomical possibilities apparent to all educated people today.

Surely our much greater knowledge of our own biology and of the physics and chemistry of the universe around us must open our eyes, to say the least, to possibilities that these ancient writers could not have envisioned. If, moreover, we have developed that awareness of a spiritual dimension, which is claimed, explicitly or otherwise, by all who talk of God and of salvation through Christ, surely we cannot be entirely insensitive to the functioning of higher intelligences in our own lives, not only as exemplars of what we may hope to become but as emissaries of God and ministers of his ever-surprising grace. The masters of Christian and other forms of spirituality have always been very much aware, of course, of the presence of beings of a higher order than we. To the extent that they have been influenced by biblical language they have called them angels.

8

PATRISTIC AND MEDIEVAL ANGELOLOGIES

It befits an angel to be in a place, yet an angel and a body are said to be in a place in quite a different sense. . . . an angel is said to be in a corporeal place by application of the angelic power in any manner whatever to any place.

ST. THOMAS, *Summa Theologiae*

The fact that allusions in the Bible to angels are so frequent made it impossible for the early Christian Fathers to neglect them. Since the Bible plainly implies their ontological reality when it does not explicitly affirm it, the early Fathers of the Church were forced to recognize them as part of their theological enterprise. Such, however, was the pressure of trinitarian and christological controversies that angelology was inevitably relegated to a minor, not to say a peripheral place. Besides, popular devotion to the angels does not seem to have developed notably until at least the later part of the fourth century. The Fathers were also near enough to the traditional polytheism of the Mediterranean world to be drawn into having to explain to their pagan antagonists that neither angels nor saints were to be worshipped as divinities and that angels, though revered for their superior status in the hierarchy of being, their closeness to God, and their benevolence to man, are nonetheless creatures like ourselves.

The notion of the incorporeality of the angels, so prominent in later medieval scholasticism, was not generally accepted until the

73

sixth century. Origen, (c.185–254), both the greatest biblical scholar and the most original mind of the patristic period, attributed to them a "subtle" or "ethereal" body. (Augustine apparently took a similar view in a later age and a very different milieu.) Origen provides a notable exception to the fact that angels were generally sidestepped in patristic enquiries, for not only did he have much to say about them; his views are also exceptionally interesting and important for an understanding of angels within the Christian tradition.

Origen, who took a universalist view of salvation, providing a schema in which even the devils, and even Satan himself, would eventually be saved, also takes the position that the angels, despite their lofty status among God's creatures, are capable of falling from their high estate. That this is to be expected would seem to follow from their having done so before, according to the ancient story of Lucifer's being ejected from heaven and drawing with him a large company of other angels who fell with him. Most of the Fathers of the Church, however, repudiated this view of Origen's as heretical, although some traces of it are to be found in some of them, such as Cyril of Jerusalem and Didymus.

Origen affirms the foregoing view in his chief philosophical work, *De Principiis,* in which he not only provides logical reasons why angels must be susceptible to a fall but adduces scriptural texts in support of his conclusion.[1] Angels derive their position or rank according to their merit. Origen's vision is of a state of affairs in which *all* creatures, be they angels or humans, may be advanced by reason of their merits or degraded because of their demerits. Angels are neither impeccable nor unredeemable. Since they are subject to the same moral laws to which humans are also subject, there is always hope for the worst of them, while even the best of them dare not rest on their oars as if a birthright grant made them eternally secure in their glory.[2] At the end of the same chapter he reverts to the question of bodies. All creatures, he says, must have bodies, for the property of being incorporeal belongs to God alone as ontologically unique; but as our human bodies in the future state of glory may be far finer and purer than those we now have, so we may think of the angels as so embodied not in flesh and blood but in embodiments of much finer nature.[3]

Nor do the angels have their special functions assigned to them by chance or arbitrary fiat. Noting from the Book of Enoch that specific functions are given to particular angels,[4] he affirms that all this is done according to merit: they receive their assignments as we might expect to receive them, that is, because they have attained a certain proficiency in a certain field that makes them equipped for a particular duty and efficient at a certain kind of task.[5] In the same chapter he discusses pre-existence and transmigration of souls and adopts a strong stand on freedom of choice. It is freedom of choice that governs the lot and the position of all of us, angels and men.[6]

The importance of such views in Origen for our present concern lies in the fact that Origen, instead of separating angels from humans as though they were subject to an entirely different order of things, embraces both under the working of the same principle. Angels are more highly evolved but they belong to the same stream of life as we do. This is a remarkable insight in terms of his age. It is highly relevant to the kind of view that I think we must take if we are to discuss angels intelligibly in the light of modern knowledge.

Origen also treats the notion of guardian angels,[7] recognizing in the old tradition about them an important truth: we are both tempted by evil spirits and guided and guarded by good ones, even by one specific angel assigned to everyone as his or her protector. This recognition of another dimension of being impinging upon the one in which habitually we live and must live on this earth is important in opening up the possibility of dimensions of existence that may lie close to us and exercise greater power over us, for good and ill, than we commonly perceive. In this chapter he also once again reminds us of the role of the freedom of the will. He later returns also to the influence that spirits exercise over us and of the need, therefore, for our watchfulness.[8]

Indeed, so strong is Origen's interest in angels that it is hardly too much to say that the whole of this, his major philosophical work, depends in considerable measure on the angelology it contains. It is inseparable from his other characteristic teachings about the pre-existence of the soul and the freedom of the will. It fits the reincarnationist schema that his entire system implies.

In the New Testament are to be found two separate enumerations of ranks or orders of angels.[9] Together these provided the Principalities, Powers, Dominions, Virtues, and Thrones that were eventually to be included in the nine orders of the angelic hosts recognized by medieval lore. To them could be added, with scriptural warrant, seraphim, cherubim, archangels, and angels, making nine in all.

To the mystical theologian named Dionysius who flourished about the year 500 is generally attributed the arranging of the angelic orders into a hierarchy consisting of nine orders of three choirs each and ranked as follows: (1) seraphim, cherubim, thrones; (2) dominations, virtues, powers; (3) principalities, archangels, angels. This Dionysius was widely believed through the Middle Ages to have been Dionysius the Areopagite whom Paul converted at Athens (Acts 17:34), despite the rejection of this identification by Hypatius, who was Bishop of Ephesus in the second quarter of the sixth century. He is known to scholars today as Dionysius the Pseudo-Areopagite or (less pedantically and more conveniently) the Pseudo-Dionysius, to distinguish him from the New Testament one. His association with the latter, however, gave him a remarkable prestige in the Middle Ages and he exercised a great influence on medieval thought, both in the East and in the West, and on the great Christian mystical traditions.[10] His own thought was notably Neo-Platonic: indeed a sort of christianized Neo-Platonism.

John Scotus Erigena (c. 810–877) used the Dionysian delineation of the celestial hierarchy. In treating angels under the second of the modes of being in his principal work *On the Division of Nature,* he paved the way for the development of the notion of angels as incorporeal beings and "separate intelligences." Albertus Magnus and Bonaventure foreshadowed the view of Thomas Aquinas that became standard in later medieval treatment of the question and indeed, for Thomists, has remained so.

According to Thomas Aquinas (1225–1274), angels constitute an order of entirely incorporeal beings. He begins his discussion of the subject by entertaining the objection of John of Damascus (c. 675–749), a Greek theologian of great historical importance, whom he quotes as asserting that while an angel may be said to be incorporeal *as regards us* he is corporeal when compared to God. That would suggest of course some sort of "subtle" body such as Origen had in mind. Noting too that John of Damascus says that an angel is an ever-movable intellectual substance, Thomas reminds us that according to Aristotle nothing is moved except a body, so it might well be objected that an angel therefore must be in some way or other a corporeal substance. Thomas, however, brushes aside such objections. First he quotes the Psalmist (Ps. 103:4) who affirms that God "makes his angels spirits." Then he argues that since intellect is superior to sense, there must be some incorporeal realities that only the intellect can apprehend and that are, in effect, therefore wholly incapable of being apprehended in any way by the senses.[11] He goes on to defend the view that angels do not belong to a species as do, say, humans and dogs, but each is a separate substance so that no angel can belong with another to any species.[12] He also holds that angels are incorruptible.[13] In spite of their incorporeal nature, angels can assume bodies,[14] since the scriptural account of Abraham's entertaining angels makes this plain and this interpretation is supported by Augustine.

The medieval schoolmen, in treating a topic, often do so in a way that tends to exhaust modern patience. Thomas considers, for example, whether an angel, not having a body, can "be in a place" and he replies affirmatively. An angel, being incorporeal, cannot be said to occupy space in the way in which a body may be said to do so; for a body occupies space by its "dimensive quantity," while an angel, being incorporeal, occupies space by the power of his presence.[15] Then can an angel be in several places at once? No, only God can be everywhere. An angel is finite, so his power can extend to only one determined thing at a time.[16] Can more than one angel be at the same time in the same place? No, because one angel, in virtue of his power, fills the place where he is.[17]

The entire treatise on the angels, consisting as it does of fifteen separate discussions, is of considerable interest in showing how the later medieval mind came to its understanding of the angels. Thomas's treatment is, as usual, masterly in terms of the way in which philosophical problems had come to be posed in his day. The notion of individuality had not yet been properly evolved, although Duns Scotus (c. 1264–1308), the last of the great medieval schoolmen, was to introduce it in his doctrine of "thisness" *(haecceitas)*. A particular human being was seen as only an example, an instance of humanity, somewhat as a particular chocolate candy is an example of what the mould whence it comes can do. The particular candy may have some accidental features, but its most notable characteristic is conformity to the mould from which it has issued. Such individuality as human beings could have was therefore seen as limited. It would have seemed to Thomas and the schoolmen generally that some kind of finite being above man was a metaphysical necessity. Angels provided exactly what was needed and apart from their seeming philosophical necessity, the Bible abundantly attested to their existence.

For Thomas, then, each angel is a "subsistent form" and each is a distinct species in himself, different from every other. Immortal and incorruptible, an angel occupies no space in the sense that bodies do, but can move wherever he decides to go and act wherever he decides to be.

Scotus follows Thomas in regarding angels as incorporeal beings and in much else concerning them; but unlike Thomas, who held that they are forms without matter (in the Aristotelian sense), Scotus contended that they are composite beings having both form and matter, although the matter is not corporeal.

How does the angelic mind work? What form does its knowing take? Does an angel reason or is his knowledge entirely intuitive? Augustine had already discussed such questions[18] and had affirmed that angels come to their knowledge of God not by audible words but directly, intuitively, by the presence of God in their souls. Thus, too, they know other creatures and they know themselves better in God than they can know themselves in themselves. Their knowledge of themselves, he says in a dramatic figure, is "twilight" knowledge *(scientia vespertina),* while their knowledge of God is "morning" knowledge *(scientia matutina),* being fuller and brighter. Thomas, in following this view in general, insisted that the angelic mode of knowledge is direct and intuitive, but Scotus opposed that view, holding that angels can reason. The schoolmen generally taught that the angels were created at the same time.

As we already noted in Chapter 4, the twelfth-century Honorius of Autun taught that each soul at the moment of conception is given into the charge of a particular guardian angel. Thomas, following Honorius in this belief, held, however, that only the lowest order of angels so functions, while Scotus taught that any angel in the celestial hierarchy might be so assigned. In 1670 Pope Clement X authorized a feast day on which the guardian angels should be honored by the whole Church: October 2.

Medieval people, especially under the influence of Saint Thomas, were programmed to regard angels as a separate order of existence to which human beings could never hope to attain. The beatified saints in heaven would indeed enjoy the vision of God and know God as we cannot know him now, even in mystical ecstasy, which at best could be but a foretaste of that beatific vision. In that blessed state they would be perfectly happy, enjoying total bliss beyond our imagining. Thomas dealt with difficult questions: "Some who go to heaven are great saints, while others get there only by the skin of their teeth. How can all be equally rewarded?" Thomas skillfully replied that the beatified would be in this respect like cups: some would be larger cups than others, but every cup would be perfectly full; that is, the most and the least magnanimous souls would be as happy as they could possibly be, as happy as they were capable of being, since each would be completely full of happiness. That is a beautiful concept indeed; but like other medieval concepts of heaven it provided no room for growth. The cups could never be enlarged.

Paradox, however, attends the way in which medieval treatments of this kind were developed. For instance, Michael is acclaimed as "Prince of the heavenly hosts," and indeed he does seem to have a certain pre-eminence in the Bible; but in the *Celestial Hierarchy* of the Pseudo-Dionysius, archangels are the second lowest in rank among the nine ranks of angels, and Michael is recognized as of that status. Well might one ask: Is it not unseemly, to say the least, to have a mere archangel at the head of the celestial armies? Mightn't it even be almost like having a corporal in charge of the United States Army? Commissioned officers generally, to say nothing of general officers, would surely find that intolerable. Are angels so gifted in humility that they gladly accept such arrangements?

We already noted in Chapter 2 an even more remarkable paradox: Mary is recognized as Queen of the Angels. In spite of her unique status as *Theotokos, Dei Genetrix,* "the God-bearer," she is nevertheless *de fide* human. Corporeally assumed into heaven though she has been acclaimed (by Pius XII in 1950), she is and never can be angelic, since angels belong to a different order of existence from humans. Yet she, in all her corporeality, reigns over the angels in all their incorporeality.

No great harm could have been done to the majority of people by inconsistencies such as we have just considered, which trouble only philosophers and (if only now and then) theologians. The lack of an evolutionary principle, however, did have at least one unspeakably horrific result. Since angels were accounted a separate order of creation antecedent to man and immortal (i.e., inextinguishable) and the human soul was likewise accounted immortal, what must happen to those men and women who end their lives in such a way that they must be forever excluded from the grace and mercy of God? So excluded, they would be left to Satan and his infernal denizens. Since Satan is not going to change, they would be forever in his power and, as Dante portrayed their destiny in his inscription on the gates of hell, forever without hope. The word used in the New Testament *(aiōnios)* is not properly translated as either "eternal" or "everlasting," but, rather, "enduring" or "age-long"; nevertheless it was so translated and so understood by learned and unlearned alike. Moreover, in the absence of any reincarnationist doctrine to provide further opportunities for working out one's salvation by God's grace in other lives, one's everlasting destiny was determined by one little life of indefinite duration.

The learned interpreted the essence of hell, the *poena damni,* to consist in the pain of having forever lost God. Nevertheless they provided ample support for the monstrous visions of everlasting torture that were presented in innumerable ways in popular preaching and in sacred art. The imaginations of ordinary men and women, devout or otherwise, were fired by unspeakably cruel pictures and terrifyingly vivid descriptions of the everlasting torments of the damned. Looking at the former and reading the latter one has the impression of looking less at speculation about the unhappier aspect of the afterlife than at media for wallowing in sado-masochistic perversion. We hear of men and women being roasted on one side for thousands of years and then turned for some thousands of years more on the other. Devils leer or howl with laughter as they chew their victims, drill holes into them, lash them with whips, boil them in cauldrons, suffocate them in boxes, and in every conceivable way cause incessant and excruciating agony to their victims.

Worse still, ancient and medieval Christian writers assure us that this state of affairs in hell brings no compassion to the minds or hearts of the righteous. On the contrary, the blessed in heaven gaze with satisfaction on such hellish scenes. Cruelty and violence seem to have been as standard ingredients in entertainment in the ancient and medieval world as they are today on popular television programs. Tertullian, in the second century, promises his readers better entertainment in the afterlife than in any show to be found on earth.[19] In the thirteenth century, Thomas Aquinas, one of the most judicious of thinkers, tells us quite explicitly that "the saints will rejoice in the punishment of evildoers."[20]

Nor can we suppose that all these horrors died with the end of the Middle Ages. Far from it. Hell in all its monstrous cruelty was one of the medieval doctrines that were carried in full strength and sharp relief right on into the nineteenth century and even beyond it and into our own. In this respect Lutheran and Calvinistic doctrine was virtually indistinguishable from Roman Catholic teaching. After the passing of the age of the classical Reformation Fathers, hell remained a popular sermon topic in Presbyterian, Methodist, Salvationist, and many other circles. Echoes of it still may be heard wherever the notion can command a hearing. For it is part of the traditional power structure of the Church, which attracts too many power maniacs into its ministry. No institution likes to be dispensable. By depriving the Church of indispensability one does much to remove its *raison d'être,* as traditionally conceived. At the least it is enfeebled in such a way as to make it look emasculated, even ridiculous, almost like a court that has authority to try cases but no power to deliver sentence. For if the Church is to function as the unique instrument of God in the world, which is both the classical Catholic and the classical Reformation view of its purpose, then it must reflect something of the power that is pre-eminent in the traditional attributes of God as depicted in the historic Christian creeds.

Probably nothing more astonishes the modern reader of medieval literature on angels than the confidence with which so many of the writers treat angels as though one could discuss them as zoologists and entomologists inventory and catalogue their specimens. The medieval mind did work along lines that seem alien to many of us today. The Renaissance of humane learning and the Reformation (which was among other things a renaissance of biblical learning) immensely changed the perspectives and the perceptions of those whom these movements affected. So let us now look at how angels fare in literature from the end of the Middle Ages to our own time. Plainly we must confine ourselves to representative examples. When, however, we turn in the next chapter to that long intervening period, we may be surprised in other ways, not least by the diversity of attitudes to the subject. We shall find, for instance, that distinguished eighteenth-century Swedish scientist, Emanuel Swedenborg, talking of angels as his daily companions and telling us of the language they use. We shall find also, half a century or so later, the English mystical poet and artist, William Blake, full of visions of angels. Perhaps even more striking still, we shall find in the long and varied Victorian age a vast stream of poets, many of whom no literary critic would call "religious" in any conventional sense of the term, alluding to angels as an indispensable symbol for use in the writer's craft. Most striking of all, we shall find, on the whole, more preoccupation with angels in the "secular" literature of this period than among theologians.

9

ANGELS IN LATER LITERATURE

But so great is the power of the angels in the spiritual world that if I should make known all that I have witnessed in regard to it it would exceed belief. Any obstruction there that ought to be removed because it is contrary to Divine order the angels cast down or overthrow merely by an effort of the will and a look.
EMANUEL SWEDENBORG, *Heaven and Its Wonders and Hell,* s. 229

John Calvin (1509–1564), the most incisive systematic theologian in the Reformation heritage, had very definite views on almost everything he discussed. He does not neglect angels but disposes of the subject rather perfunctorily. After a characteristically emphatic proclamation of the sovereignty of God he announces that he proposes to discuss the nature of man but feels that first he "ought to insert something concerning angels."[1] Then, noting that Moses, in his account of creation,[2] "accommodating himself to the rudeness of the common folk, mentions . . . no other works of God than those which show themselves to our own eyes. Yet afterward when he introduces angels as ministers of God, one may easily infer that he to whom they devote their effort and functions is their Creator." Then after a predictable warning against attributing to them any reflection, even, of divinity and a reminder that they are but creatures, he deplores all speculation about angels as "unprofitable." While he cannot, of course, ignore the many references to angels in the Bible and he does recognize that they are indeed ontological realities, not mere human imaginings,[3] he urges his readers not to inquire into "ob-

82

scure matters" or about "anything except what has been imparted to us by God's Word."[4]

Of course Calvin's repetitious emphases on the sovereignty of God are salutary and, insofar as we can believe that he was really confronting some polytheistic tendency in his audience, important. They would be even more salutary were it not that they imply an approach to Bible reading that almost all learned Calvinists today abjure as uncritical if not naive. Calvin, although his language on the subject of angels must sound dogmatic, not to say arrogant, to most educated ears today, was by no means alone among classical theologians in his treatment of angels. For although St. Thomas, for example, does treat the subject with care and does provide an angelology of great merit in terms of the thought of his age, the mainstream of Christian theology has generally skirted around the subject rather than addressed it. Most theologians have been content to recount what scriptural or other "authority" dictates on the subject and then to steer clear of it as if they found in it a *soupçon* of theological embarrassment. Calvin, indeed, seems less inclined to reticence when he comes to the Devil and his works. Here again he is but following a general trend in classical theologies, Catholic and Reformed. By and large we find comparatively little inclination in the mainstream of classical Reformation thought to deal with angels at all.

Of course there are exceptions. Luther, in a Michaelmas sermon, referred to his "guides, the holy angels." Bullinger, likewise following the traditional medieval language here, says that "our translation to heaven is brought about by angels carrying up our souls with a most swift flight."[5] Generally speaking, however, such allusions by theologians and popular preachers merely echo the traditional language of Catholic piety. Angels do not loom large in the theology of the Reformation heritage and when we do find them noticed we rarely find them discussed at any length unless (as we have seen in Calvin) with a caution against misuse of the concept.

We hear plenty, however, of one class of angel: the Devil and his legions. In popular religious literature before and after the Reformation we find not only innumerable references to them but considerable detail. With that preoccupation went a belief in witchcraft, widely believed to be a manifestation of diabolical activity. The Devil was very real indeed to many. Even a young, Jesuit-educated doctor at Wells in Elizabethan times kept seeing the Devil and got rid of him only by throwing a rosary at him.[6] Both Catholic and Protestant theologians were sure of the Devil's presence and of the need to wage constant war against him, for generally speaking they were disposed to regard him as having been given a very long rope indeed to do his mischief. Only now and then do we find talk of good angels assisting in the human warfare against these demonic powers.

We fare better in the "secular" literature of the period, in which many allusions may be found such as that expressed by Horatio in his farewell to the dead Hamlet:

> Good night, sweet prince,
> And flights of angels sing thee to thy rest.

The words echo, of course, the haunting poetry of the ancient prayer in the Latin burial service which, translated, runs: "May angels conduct thee into Paradise. . . . May the choir of angels receivè thee and, with Lazarus, once a beggar, mayest thou have rest eternal."

Dante, in his great epic, had inevitably included angels: Satan at the core of the Earth and apex of hell, and multitudes of the good angels in his *Paradiso*. Milton (1608–1674) in his very different way, puts angels at the very center of his cosmic scenario. They dwell in countles multitudes in the Empyrean, a boundless region of light and freedom and joy, and live dispersed throughout it in organized ranks. Noble and free beyond human imagining, they are ready at less than a moment's notice to carry out the behests of the Almighty. Some seem to be constantly near the Throne itself, while others, such as Gabriel, are more

> conversant on Earth
> With man or men's affairs.[7]

Milton, using the old Ptolemaic astronomy that was already becoming even then *démodé,* was able to construct a magnificent, panoramic, literary map of the cosmos or, more exactly an atlas of comparative maps showing the arrangements before and after the Fall of the angels. Needless to say, Milton uses allegorical images for his celestial geography, but the angelic hosts are indubitably taken to represent a definite ontological reality apart from which any model we cared to use would radically mislead us. So important for our enterprise is Milton's treatment of angels that I shall postpone a fuller discussion of it until Chapter 17, "Angels as Andro-gyns."

Milton's Empyrean is on such a stupendous scale that we some-times get the impression that humanity, despite its importance, is almost a colonial outpost or protectorate in the infinitely vast divine empire of the angelic hosts which, with the Throne of God in its midst, is what runs the universe. Yet the very sublimity of Milton's fantasy may distance us from the reality to which, in his theologi-cally heterodox way, he plainly wished to focus our attention. Dante's vision, by contrast, had been on a more modest scale, more measured to our human limitations and therefore to many of us more effective in communicating to us the significance of the concept of angels. In both, however, angels are central in a way seldom to be found in the classical theological systems.

Paradoxical though it may seem to some, heterodoxy is often more hospitable to angels than is orthodoxy. William Blake (1757–1827), notably unconventional in his religious beliefs, was very much influenced by both Jakob Boehme (1575–1624) and Emanuel Swedenborg (1688–1772), both of whom, each in his own way and according to his own circumstance, deviated singularly from pre-vailing theological opinion. Boehme, a Lutheran by upbringing, was a mystical and theosophical writer who influenced not only much of later mystical literature in the West, especially in Germany and the English-speaking world, but thinkers such as Hegel. The son of a German farmer, he worked first as a shepherd, then as a shoe-maker.

Very different was Swedenborg's background. His father became a theological professor at Uppsala and Bishop of Skara. Emanuel, however, turned at an early age to work in paleontology and physics, showing remarkable scientific originality. He anticipated many later hypotheses and discoveries; for example, magnetic theory and the machine gun. In nebular theory he reached the hypothesis of the formation of sun and planets long before the work of Laplace. He was the first to use mercury for the air pump and he has been generally regarded as the father of crystallography. In 1714 he was appointed to a position on the Swedish Board of Mines, from which he resigned in 1747 to devote himself to studies arising out of what he claimed to be persistent communications from angels and other agencies in a spiritual world that he now took to be the key to an understanding of all scientific knowledge. Applying himself with unabated industry to his new studies, he learned Hebrew and acquired other skills for their pursuit. Although never relinquishing his interest in physics and the other natural sciences, he now devoted himself to expounding his understanding of the spiritual nature of the universe.

I have outlined the contrasting backgrounds of Boehme and Swedenborg to show how differently these two great influences on Blake's own genius had arrived at their mystical understanding of the nature of things. Blake, known to many from poems such as *Tiger, tiger, burning bright* and the famous lines that ask, in the proem to his *Milton,* whether Jerusalem could have been built amid England's "dark, satanic mills," was profoundly influenced by both Boehme and Swedenborg. Angels abound in Blake's works, both in his writings and in his drawings, and he adopts a great deal of his imagery and symbolism from both Boehme and Swedenborg, especially but by no means only from the former, whom he accounted much greater than the latter.

For instance, Boehme has three principles: heaven, hell, and our own world; and every spirit is confined in its own principle, the evil angels in hell and the good in heaven. "Thus we are to understand that the Evil and Good Angels dwell near one another, and yet there is the greatest immense Distance between them. For the *Heaven is in Hell* and the *Hell is in Heaven,* and yet the one is not manifest to the other; and although the Devil should go many Millions of Miles, desiring to enter into Heaven, and to see it, yet he would be still in Hell and not see it."[8]

So Blake, in the frontispiece of *The Marriage of Heaven and Hell,* shows each kind of spirit in its own property, the one of fire, the other of light. In a color printed drawing made a few years later and entitled simply "Good and Evil Angels," the Devil is portrayed as blind and so unable to see the Good Angel, whom he is trying to approach but cannot, because neither can perceive the other: the one because he is bathed in the light of God, the other because he is covered by blackness and encompassed by burning fire. Blake's drawing is as fit to illustrate Boehme's ideas as Blake's.

Although Blake, in the course of his own development, lost much of his interest in Swedenborg's thought, the latter's symbolism left an indelible mark upon him. In Blake's poem, *The Angel,* for instance, we read of

an Angel who had a bright key,
And he opened the coffins and set them all free.

This seems to echo a strange passage in one of Swedenborg's writings in which he reports that a spirit with a sooty face and dirty clothes expressed a great desire to be admitted to heaven. Then suddenly the angels called on him to throw off his "vile raiment" which he immediately did. Swedenborg relates that he was informed that such dark spirits, when they are being prepared for heaven, are stripped of their old clothes and, being clad in new, shining garb, become angels.[9]

As Yeats has pointed out, however, no matter what Blake borrowed from Boehme or Swedenborg, he transformed it in molding it into his own system. Blake, who was both a Platonist at heart and probably more familiar with reincarnationism and the karmic principle than were most Englishmen of his day (he had read the *Bhagavad-Gita,* for instance), saw angels, good and evil, as the real forces behind the foibles and the triumphs, the enslavements and the liberations, of mortal men and women. Our human battles, great or petty, arise from our anger, avarice, and lust. These spiritual diseases are not necessarily fatal; they bring us back over and over again to the scene of our preoccupation with them till we can discard the filthy rags of our bondage and be clothed in the habiliments of light. So in the face of a little child he sees the angelic light. His entire scheme, with all its difficulties and phantasmagoria, is based upon a view that had its roots in Plato and ran through a long philosophical tradition extending all the way to Berkeley (1685–1753), and pointing to a spiritual reality in which forces higher than ourselves are constantly at work, whether we notice it or not.

Such a vision may be expressed in a large variety of ways, but the essential theme is the same: we customarily look at the world around us half-blinded by our own spiritual disorders which actually hide the realities from us. We cannot see clearly what is going on. We cannot see where the action truly is. It is in forces far superior to man where the warfare between good and evil is being waged. Blake, indebted as he was to Swedenborg, saw angels as the symbols of these forces. Orthodox theologians, Christian and Jewish, have generally tended to suspect anything that seemed to challenge the monotheistic emphasis.

Swedenborg, to whom Blake was so much indebted (as Joyce was indebted to the Jesuits for his conceptualizations), was a visionary who used the concept of angels to bring the nature and the vitality of the spiritual world alive to a society (and not least to an ecclesiastical organization) that had all but lost sight of the reality of the spiritual realm. According to him, angels, however conceived, are indeed ontological realities far superior to humankind. They are able to communicate wisdom only because in the first place they have become capable of receiving it and they have become capable of receiving it only "because their interiors are open."[10]

Perhaps no one in the history of humankind has written about angels with such matter-of-fact nonchalance as has Swedenborg. In the latter part of his life he lived in a world peopled with angels. It was a world in many ways strangely like the one with which we are familiar, yet one in which the spiritual state of the inhabitants dictates the entire scenario. It is the combination of the familiar and the unfamiliar that at first startles us as we come to grips with Swedenborg's writings about the angelic world. The angels do not only speak; they write. Angelic writing is very different from human writing; for example, he tells us, in the inmost or highest heaven the angels express affections with vowels; with consonants they express the ideas that spring from the affections; and with words they express the total communication that they wish to make. He assures us that in angelic language a few words can express what it takes pages of human writing to say. Angelic writing reflects, moreover, the extraordinarily ductile quality of angelic speech. Angelic speech is audible, for angels, like ourselves, have mouths and tongues and ears. They breathe, too; but all this occurs in a spiritual atmosphere adapted to their angelic nature. The tones of their speech reflect their affections, the words or vocal articulations correspond to the thoughts that spring from their affections. Yet he goes on to tell us that, having conversed often with angels, sometimes as friend to friend, sometimes as stranger to stranger, angelic language has nothing in common with human language except that their sounds are the sounds of specific affections. Angels cannot speak human language. It is impossible for them to do so not only because it is too cumbersome and discursive, but because they can utter only that which expresses with perfect sincerity the love that is in them, whence issues their grandeur, their beauty, and their power. Angelic speech, he says, is an indescribable symphony.[11]

Angels, however, as Swedenborg depicts them, have no power of themselves. They are but agents of the Almighty, the Eternal One. If an angel were to doubt whence his power comes he would instantly become so weak that he could not resist a single evil spirit. "For this reason angels ascribe no merit whatever to themselves, and are averse to all praise and glory on account of anything they do, ascribing all the praise and glory to the Lord."[12]

What is evident over and over again in Swedenborg is that the angels in the spiritual world, although they are ordered in various ranks, are all real entities and far superior to man. He does not invent a race of imaginary beings for the composition of a poetic allegory. To back up his own experience of how the spiritual world impinges on the empirical one he quotes the Bible: "David saw the angel that smote the people."[13]

Man has freedom, according to Swedenborg, but only because of the equilibrium of heaven and hell between which he is poised. This God-given freedom makes it possible for humanity, which is born into a morass of evils of every sort, to be redeemed by love, which makes possible our liberation from bondage.[14] This liberation is not easily attained, however, for the love that effects it entails sacrifice: the sacrifice of self. But if love entails such a sacrifice, surely the angels can be no strangers to it, being plainly within its swirl.

The ancient Judaeo-Christian traditions concerning angelology have lingered long in literature, often in not particularly expected places. The concept of the guardian angel is especially tenacious. Browning, in a poem entitled *The Guardian Angel,* asks the angel, when he has done with a child, to take over the charge of the poet: a quaint literary conceit. Robert Burton, in *The Anatomy of Melancholy,* for long a much-read classic, affirms that everyone has a good and a bad angel, in lifelong attendance "on him in particular." Sir Thomas Browne has a good deal to say about angels in his *Religio Medici,* and at least two of his major critics, Alexander Ross and Sir Kenelm Digby, took him to task on minute points in his allusions to them. Longfellow wrote of "the language spoken by angels." Leigh Hunt, in his lovely poem, *Abou Ben Adhem,* has Abou wake to find an angel writing "in a book of gold" the names of all those who love God. Abou asks if his name is there and the angel answers no. Then Abou, speaking more softly but still with cheer, asks that the angel write him down as one who loves his fellow men. The angel departs and returns the next night showing Abou the names of those whom God had specially blest, "And lo! Ben Adhem's name led all the rest."

This is a typical example of the Victorian use of angels as intermediaries between man and the God who reigns in light inaccessible, his face perpetually hid by the seraphim. William

Alexander, another Victorian, in a poem celebrating the mystery of Oxford, notes that on her "pale brow are looks of youth," yet "angels listening on the argent floor" know of her continuous life throughout the near-millennium of her antiquity. Angels not only surprise us with visitations; they listen under the floorboards and in the walls, hearing as clearly from high heaven as in the silence behind a rock in a lonely desert. Anyone who thinks that angels died with the passing of the Middle Ages should be prepared to witness their resurrection in literature in the humanistic Renaissance and their persistence from the sixteenth century down to our own time. The angel is, to say the least, an indispensable literary symbol even for those poets and other writers whom we would not normally dub "religious." As one of the later Victorians, Francis Thompson, wrote, the angels do indeed still "keep their ancient places." They most certainly have done so in the best of European and American literature.

Before going on to our next topic, we shall find it worthwhile to devote a few moments' reflection to the comparative absence of angels from the writings of the great Christian mystics. For surely, absent though they be from the mainstream of orthodox theological discussion, we might expect to find them emerging in full splendor in one or other of the great schools of Christian mysticism. But that is not at all what we find. Why, then, are the pages of the writings of men such as Boehme, Swedenborg, and Blake, all indisputably heterodox in their own respective circumstances and so generally regarded ever since, filled with talk of angels, while we hear so little talk of such entities in the writings of the acknowledged masters of the spiritual life that have been accepted in one way or another within the framework of Christian orthodoxy? Why do we hear so little of them, for example, among the Spanish mystics such as Teresa? In the works of the fourteenth-century Jan van Ruysbroeck we might surely expect much about angels, since he is reputed to have been so much influenced by the Pseudo-Dionysius, but in *The Seven Steps of the Ladder of Spiritual Love* are to be found only the most casual references to angels in the Fifth Step, where, moreover, we are informed that the highest ranks of angels (Thrones, Cherubim, and Seraphim) "do not join in our struggle against our vices, but dwell with us only when, above all conflict, we are with God in peace, in contemplation, and in perennial love."[15] Only the lower orders of angels assist in our struggles and even they are but cursorily mentioned. Francis of Sales (1567–

1622), who may be said to have popularized the cultivation of the interior life among worldly people, virtually ignores angels in his long-popular *Introduction to the Devout Life.*

One of the most profoundly interesting mystical writers in Christian history is Catherine of Genoa (1447–1510), a married lady of noble Ligurian family. Her mystical writings are the subject of an extensive study by Baron Friedrich von Hügel (1852–1925),[16] a learned Roman Catholic layman sympathetic to the Modernist movement in the Church of his day. Even Catherine's work contains little on angels, although one of her favorite terms is *presenza* ("presence"—she wrote in Italian), which comes straight out of the tradition of the Pseudo-Dionysius.[17] This emphasis and the term expressing it goes back to the Neo-Platonists and indeed even to the Greek Mysteries, where a god could suddenly enter and take part in the sacred dance. In Dionysius, "choirs" of angelic dancers might attend such an illuminating experience of the divine presence, yet Catherine makes no mention of them.[18]

The reasons for such widespread reticence about angels among such acknowledged masters of Christian spirituality are no doubt complex. Some, however, are easily detectable. Although belief in angels is indeed officially taught as *de fide* and therefore would seem to be even more likely to be found in the mainstream of Christian mysticism than in heterodox writers such as Boehme and Blake, the opposite is the case. The Church's developed teaching on the nature and status of angels must have sounded vaguely unintelligible at best and, at worst, thoroughly confusing. Even more significantly, perhaps, angels had become so remote that, even with occasional assurances that at least the lower ranks of angels did sometimes assist humans in their tribulations and struggles, the ordinary men or woman could not but feel, however unconsciously, that such essentially different and exalted beings could not really be expected to understand either human shortcomings or human woes.

Theoretically, Christ was of course best fitted for that, since according to the great Council of Chalcedon in 451 he had been declared to be both fully divine and fully human. In practice, however, Christ's humanity gradually receded in popular Catholic devotion throughout the Middle Ages and by the time of Michelangelo he could be depicted in that great artist's famous painting as the stern Divine Judge. So since the humanity of Christ had been obscured in popular piety and since the Church taught that the angels never had any humanity to lose, the task of supporting us poor mortals in our struggles and interceding for us in our plight had to be shouldered by the saints who, after all, had known the torments and temptations of the flesh as well as the angers and cruelties of the human spirit in its rebellion against God. By and large medieval people were earthier than we are today. Angels might command a formal nod of respect, but saints evoked love. According to traditional teaching one could hope to become a saint (in heaven if not before) but in no way could one ever become an angel.

10

ANGELS IN THE VISUAL ARTS

The man who never in his mind
and thought travelled to
heaven is no artist.
WILLIAM BLAKE

ngels, as we have seen in an earlier chapter, are thoroughly biblical and well recognized in Jewish lore. We must not expect, however, to see them depicted in Jewish settings, for Orthodox Judaism takes very literally the commandment that bans the making of any "graven image" (Exodus 20:4). Although, as we shall see, angels play a prominent role in Muslim teaching, we rarely find them in Islamic art, which inherits the same restrictions against representational decoration. There are, however, notable exceptions. In the manuscript collection in the University of Edinburgh there is a depiction of Gabriel appearing to Muhammad. The example shown in the present book, depicting the Annunciation in Muslim fashion (Figure 28), is another such exception. Generally speaking, however, in Western art the portrayal of angels has been left almost entirely to those artists and sculptors who can make full use of the freedom that Christian custom affords them. For a comparative example, however, of Hellenistic, Islamic, and Christian representations, see Figure 34.

Although it is in the Catholic tradition that the Church has most bountifully patronized the visual arts, by no means does every

93

painting of an angel come from a Catholic brush or every angelic sculpture emerge from a Catholic chisel. Rembrandt (1606–1669), whose paintings include several angelic scenes, was of the Dutch Reformed heritage. (His affair with a servant girl who bore him a child scandalized the strait-laced churchfolk of Amsterdam, but that made him no less Protestant than many a medieval Italian painter was Catholic.) Dürer (1471–1528), although he never formally left the Roman Catholic Church, was sympathetic to the Reformation and was eulogized by Luther. Still, when all that is said, it remains true that angels have been painted and sculpted more often than not under a Catholic sun.

That does not mean, of course, that we must go to Roman Catholic churches to find them. We shall find them abundantly in Eastern Orthodox ones, which are often much enriched by icons, many of which represent angels. For in spite of the ban against three-dimensional art in that tradition, iconography has played a special role in its devotional life and angels are a favorite subject. We need not go to any church, however, to see angels in art. One cannot walk very far through the great art galleries of Europe or America without seeing them abundantly displayed. They seem to be as much at home, moreover, in these "secular" surroundings as in any church; perhaps even more so. For the concept of the angel is not confined to any particularly theological atmosphere; it is an archetype deeply embedded in the minds of ordinary men and women, often in ways that seem independent of any discernible religious faith.

Angels in art appear in a dazzlingly varied array of guises. Frequently the artist shows them as idealized human beings, very often indeed otherwise indistinguishable from the rest of us except for the wings and even these are sometimes absent. Their faces occasionally reflect their provenance: the country of their origin and the artist's own milieu. Some of Dürer's are noticeably Germanic and some of Rembrandt's distinctly Dutch. The angels in the engravings of Johann Ulrich Krauss (1645–1719) in the first edition of his *Biblisches Engel-u. Kunstwerck* fit smoothly into the vintage Augsburg baroque of their surroundings. All this is to be expected, for after all angels are nothing if not highly sensitive beings who inevitably pick up the vibrations of the atmosphere wherever they go, so if you see one in Lapland you can hardly expect the same sort of manifestation that you would see in Ravenna or Rome.

Many angels are highly stylized in art; others are more naturalistic. Others again, such of those by Jan van Eyck (1385–1441) and his brother Hubert (died 1426) in their works such as the *Adoration* and the altarpiece at Ghent (Figure 37) seem to combine the stylized, allegorizing treatment characteristic of the medieval tradition with a naturalism that was uncommon if not entirely new to their age. Sometimes angels are shown in vast numbers whirling in heaven. In Doré's illustrations to Cantos 27 and 31 of Dante's *Paradiso,* for instance, the countless hosts of them are displayed in this way with great elegance. In the second of these two they magnificently form a celestial rose. Sometimes, as in Cimabue (1240–1320), they are in attendance on the Blessed Virgin, their queen. Elsewhere they may be depicted as scurrying earthward in great haste to rescue a human in need. Often they are depicted as joyful, perhaps singing the *Gloria in excelsis.* Very often they are playing the lute or some other musical instrument (sometimes a stringed instrument, sometimes a woodwind) as in the buxom angel in a fresco by Melozzo da Forli (1438–1494) in the sacristy of St. Peter's, Rome. So also in a painting of the Presentation by Vittore Carpaccio (1460–1522) in the Accademia in Venice, where a very human-looking angel lacking visible wings is plucking the strings of an instrument almost as large as herself, which she has poised between her chin and her knee. Hans Memling (1430–1494), whose work often combines a serious-minded Flemish mystical quality with a carefree Italian grace, has a charming painting of a celestial concert in which each of the angels is playing a different instrument. Some interpret the wind instrument as symbolic of the breathing in and out of the divine Wisdom. Music is the most "disembodied" of the arts, being almost pure form, as are the angels themselves in medieval philosophy.

Yet angels in art are not always joyful or making sweet music. Giotto (1266–1337) painted a fresco in Padua that includes angels wringing their hands and weeping in grief at the death of Christ. (Figure 23.) The fifteenth-century Carlo Crivelli pursues a similar motif and Filippino Lippi (1457–1504) has a striking picture of a sorrowing angel. Dürer has a woodcut showing an angel with raised sword expelling Adam and Eve from the Garden of Eden, reminding us that angels do not merely laugh or weep; they have work to do and some of it is disciplinary. (See also his *Apocalypse,* Figure 18.) Although some angels come in richly embroidered copes and other ecclesiastical vestments, others are casually dressed in the everyday clothes familiar to the artist who painted them. Murillo (1618–1682) has a painting in the Louvre in which angels, so casually attired, are working at various typical kitchen chores, preparing their meal. Yet they are not necessarily at their most captivating when they come in such casual clothing or at such workaday chores. Surely never could an angel be more angelic than the one portrayed by Fra Angelico (1387–1455) in a work also in the Louvre in which St. Dominic and a group of his brethren, each seated at table in the white habit and black mantilla of their Order, are being served by two winged angels, magnificently robed in rich blue and gold, each with a little gold halo, meekly and gently bringing food to the friars' table with simple dignity as if in imitation of the humility of Christ. Not only do we find here celebrated the dignity of manual labor; the mystery of the Incarnation itself shines through the blue and scarlet and gold of their modest-sized wings.

In a very different style nearer to our own times we find a *gouache* by George Rouault, who was born in 1871 in a cellar while the house was shaking under shellfire in the Franco-Prussian War. Here a rather ungainly guardian angel hovers beside a huddle of no less graceless children, towering above them yet bending tenderly toward them. Despite such changes in style, however, from the angels of Byzantine art down to the present day the basic concept of angels remains much the same. I have already suggested that the sensitivity of angels causes them to pick up the vibrations of the places they visit. No less, then, may we expect them to pick up the beat of the times.

Devils also are portrayed in a wide variety of ways. They are usually very easily recognized, although, as we shall presently see, there are exceptions. They often have wings, sometimes bat-like, but again not necessarily so. In Figure 32 we even find one with a halo. (The reason for this is that originally the halo was an emblem not of holiness but of power, of which the devils have plenty.) They often have horns, but again they may not. In *The Temptation of Christ* by Duccio di Buoninsegna (1260–1320) Satan is bearded and winged but without horns. Signorelli's (c. 1450–1523) devil, bald, horned, and leering cruelly and hideously as he carries off a woman to hell astride his enormous wingspan, with her hands firmly secured in his, is horrific enough without that further negative embellishment. Nor has he the cloven feet that according to some sources are said to be the "sure giveaway" that devils have difficulty in hiding. (See Figure 9.)

Fallen angels in art can be as attractive, however, as the good ones. In an illustration for *Paradise Lost* (after a sculpture by Darodes), Satan and Belzebuth, in consultation on strategy for war, are shown as full-bodied, muscular, handsome young men, scantily clad and, except for the wings, indistinguishable from human males. The fifteenth-century La Sassetta depicts St. Anthony encountering, by the wayside near his cell, a devil cleverly disguised as a female angel, neatly winged and with her hands demurely folded across her breast. This sort of ruse, as we saw earlier, is a favorite ploy of devils.

The good angels are engaged in such a variety of beneficent tasks and have so many different functions in the service of God that one need never be astonished at the attitudes in which we find them. If they can be found cooking a meal, seemingly finding no encumbrance in their wings, we certainly ought not to wonder at finding them with the function of thurifers. Enguerrand Quarton, another fifteenth-century painter, has a delightful picture of a girlish angel blowing into a censer to ready it for the ceremony of the Coronation of the Blessed Virgin, to insure, as would any good thurifer, that it is well-enough lighted to exude smoke copiously when swung. The seventeenth-century Francisco Zurburan has a more worldly-clad angel swinging a censer, with a mixture of experienced competence and temperamental insouciance in his demeanor, and a pair of very sturdy wings on his back.

We have seen that in the celestial hierarchy that came down to the medieval thinkers, the seraphim come first and the cherubim second in rank among the nine orders. The seraphim are specifically mentioned only once in the Old Testament (Isaiah 6) and never in the New. In Christian art they are typically portrayed as beings of great splendor, ablaze with fire, full of light, and pouring forth love. They are supposed to be ceaselessly engaged in singing the Trisagion (Holy, Holy, Holy) before the Throne of God. The iconography of the cherubim is very much more varied, ranging from complex figures to the little *putti* (cherubs) with which we are all familiar. The history of this development may be summarized as follows.

The Hebrew word *cherubim* (a plural noun) means "fullness of God's knowledge." Both the name and the concept are Akkadian or

Assyrian in origin. In Akkadian *karibu* means "one who prays" or "one who communicates," and the Hebrew is connected with this word. In Assyrian art the cherubim were depicted as great winged creatures, either with human or with leonine faces and with the bodies of eagles, bulls, sphinxes, or other impressive creatures. At first they were conceived as palace or temple guardians rather than as angels. They seem to be connected, if distantly, with the Indian Garuda, a multiwinged, aquiline creature who was Krishna's mount. The iconography originated in the description provided by Ezekiel (Ezekiel 1:1-5), so that we get a tetramorph, i.e., a composite figure made up of four entities. The Apocalypse refers to this concept with its image of four beasts, six-winged and full of eyes within (Revelation 4:7–8). This representation is also of Assyrio-Babylonian origin. The four could be made to represent many things: the four winds of heaven, the four corners of the earth, the four evangelists, or what you will.

As time went on artists no doubt tired of this complicated iconographic tradition. The cherubim changed into one-headed angels and from being big angels into being little ones. They took the form of *putti* or winged children or even babies: an idea taken over in very early Christian times from Pompeiian representations. (For contrast see Figures 10 and 11.) These *putti* are called in English "cherubs," using the English instead of the Hebrew plural. They need not be miniature in size, only childlike in form and appearance. The *putti* of Bernini supporting the Holy Water stoup in St. Peter's, Rome, are gigantic. (See Figure 11.) The cherubs that we find so endearing are often chubby and pink-cheeked with irresistible smiles to enchant the spectator. Sometimes, however, they are winged heads *(psychai)* lacking bodies: a subtler portrayal of the angelic concept.

Most angels in art are unidentifiable by name. Like foot soldiers in an army, the multitudes of the heavenly hosts are hidden in anonymity. Archangels, however, being of superior rank, are usually easy to identify by name. The four mentioned in the Bible (Michael, Gabriel, Raphael, and Uriel) are distinctive enough to be generally recognizable.

Michael, after all, is commander in chief of the celestial army. Although in the Renaissance period he is very variously represented, he is always young, strong, and handsome, usually wearing a splendid coat of mail with sword, shield, and spear, all bright and shining, ready for battle. For a modern example, see Epstein's bronze in Coventry Cathedral (Figure 5). He is often seen in combat with Satan, who in this context is frequently represented as a serpent or dragon (Revelation 12:7–9). (For a probably Coptic Michael so engaged, see Figure 33.) Sometimes he is wearing a jewelled crown. His wings are generally conspicuous and very grand; but in art (especially with angels) one must always allow for the artist's personal whim, so if an aberrant painter chooses to paint him wingless, that is no proof against his identity as Michael. A medieval Russian Michael, more ruler than messenger, is shown in Figure 40.

Gabriel, as the chief ambassador of God to humanity, is most commonly shown in the pursuit of this role and therefore in the company of the recipient of one or other of his missions. In Christian art the most notable of these is, of course, the Annunciation to Mary that she is to be the Mother of the Christ (Luke 1:26–28). In earlier paintings of this great event he is usually depicted as a majestic figure, richly attired, sometimes wearing a crown and bearing a scepter: the insignia of sovereignty. His right hand is extended in salutation, while the Virgin Mary sits submissively and humbly receiving him. From about the fourteenth century, however, the roles are to some extent reversed. Mary becomes the more prominent of the two, as though already Queen of the Angels and therefore receiving Gabriel as her dutiful subject, while Gabriel carries, instead of the scepter, a lily as a symbol of the purity of the Virgin. His hands are often folded modestly on his breast. He may carry a scroll inscribed with the opening words, in Latin, of the Ave Maria. Signs of the development of the contrast appear in Figures 6, 7, and 8.

Raphael is the chief of the guardian angels; indeed he is the Guardian of all humanity. He is often depicted with Tobias, to whom he showed the fish from which were to be made potions that would cure blindness and other afflictions. (See Figure 2, which refers to the story in Tobit 5 and 6 in the Old Testament Apocrypha.) Raphael is especially solicitous for pilgrims and other wayfarers, and so is often depicted as such himself, carrying a pilgrim's staff and shod with sandals. Sometimes he has a water gourd or wallet slung from a strap over his shoulder. His demeanor is generally mild and kindly: a friendly man rather than a magnificent angel. Sometimes, however, as in Figure 3, where he is seen liberating Peter from prison (Acts 12:7–9), he can be bathed in a glow of that supernal light that all angels carry with them wherever they go, whether we mortals perceive it or not.

Raphael is assisted by innumerable helpers who come in as many guises as there are problems for angels to solve. The guardian angels have a special concern for children and therefore often come appositely in the form of children themselves, adapted (such is angelic courtesy) to the occasion. To help the aged one must become attuned to the aged, in their weakness and in their strength. Better than studying geriatrics at an institute or college, one becomes oneself, at least for the time being, an old man or woman. A good kindergarten teacher likewise becomes something of a child herself if she is to succeed in the classroom. So with the guardian angels in the service of Raphael. In watching over chidlren they assume the form of children. A charming example is shown in Figure 16: a child guardian angel in petticoats with wings as large as herself and her little head bathed in as much light as a little head could carry: just enough for the occasion. Angels always know how to dress: in rich finery or filthy rags, as befits the work they have to do at the time. Sometimes, to help us appreciate the reason for the angelic visitation, there can be detected in the background the figure of a devil, whose presence provides eloquent explanation of the reason for the angelic intervention.

Of the four biblically mentioned archangels, the least widely represented in art is Uriel. As the interpreter of prophecies, however, he is usually depicted carrying a book or a papyrus scroll. His name means "the light of God": a concept often represented by the iconographers. According to one early Christian legend, it was he who appeared to the disciples on the road to Emmaus (Luke 24:13–35) as Christ's angelic envoy. He may sometimes be seen, therefore, in that guise. In *Paradise Lost* Milton represents him as the regent of the sun.

Christian painters have no difficulty in finding suitable biblical authority for their treatment of angels in art. We must not forget, however, that some of the models they use have ancestors in pagan archetypes. The transition from ancient pagan attitudes and motifs to Christian ones was slow and, as we saw at the outset of this book, the old pagan images linger on even today. So, while the Hebrew psalmist assures us that we have nothing to fear, because God "shall give his angels charge over thee, to keep thee in all thy ways"

(Psalm 91:11), we cannot forget that other ancient peoples had models not entirely unlike the biblical ones. The ancient Romans, for instance, held that every man has his Genius to direct him and every woman her Juno to inspire her.

Many were the pagan archetypes that lay behind the representation of Christian themes: archetypes that Christian artists might sometimes disguise but often had to renounce. The ancient and very widespread cult of the great Egyptian goddess Isis, sister and wife of Osiris and mother of Horus, represented the productive force of nature. Together Isis and Osiris ruled the lower world. So popular was Isis that her cult spread to Greece, with a whole network of mysteries attached to it, and thence spread to Rome along with so many other Greek imports. Apuleius, who wrote about the middle of the second century of the Christian era, remodelled many of the ancient stories and incorporated them into his *Metamorphoses* or *Golden Ass.* The most famous and endearing tale in this collection is his "Cupid and Psyche," an allegory of the soul in relation to love. The last part refers to Isis as his helper and to his initiation into her mysteries. By the time of Apuleius, Isis was still widely worshipped and remained a powerful deity that followers of the Christian Way had to dethrone. In Figure 39 we see her in full Egyptian splendor, manifested as a winged angel, her wings spread out to gather her devotees and enfold them to her in a unifying sleep.

Christianity, as a strictly monotheistic religion, could not possibly accommodate any of the deities in any pantheon of antiquity. Their foibles and their intrigues, their lovemaking and their wars, could have no more place in Christianity than in Judaism or (later on) in Islam. What could Christianity do with, say, a Venus who became jealous of the beauty of Psyche and sent Cupid to make her fall in love with a grotesque creature? Or with a Cupid who outsmarted Venus by falling in love with Psyche himself? Nothing. The old pagan gods and goddesses had to go. They could be *transformed,* however, into agencies of the One True God, the Eternal, the Almighty, the Invisible One, the Creator of all things, visible and invisible. Through the Christian use of art, the iconographers could conduct the transformation with decorum and grace and so, instead of imposing a total ban on the use of art (as some indeed sought to do at one stage), the Church not only permitted but encouraged the transformation of the most powerful of the ancient archetypes in such a way as to make possible their enlistment in the army of the One True God. The angels provided one of the most ductile of the media available for this process.

As the Christian Church gradually established herself throughout Europe, slowly moving northward, art became the chief instrument of evangelization. It acquired this role not merely because for a long time few people outside the ranks of monks and nuns and clerics could read, but because the power of the ancient archetypes was, and indeed remains, so immense that they could not be ignored. Poets, painters, and sculptors could and did use their talents abundantly for the necessary transformation. In the liturgy all the five senses were assailed. They served as five spearheads in the assault by the armies of the Lord against the obstacles so copiously provided by the World, the Flesh, and the Devil. So High Mass became and has remained one of the great art forms of Europe: a liturgical dance ablaze with color and movement and light, with sweet-smelling incense rising heavenward, and with noble and chaste music floating through the air like the angels who are so emphatically alluded to in song at the very heart of the Sacred Mysteries. Such is the variety of functions that fall within the purview of the angels that they can be called in for almost any imaginable emergency and for any kind of task.

Do we need to remind people of God's personal care and love for each one of us, even for the sparrow that falls to the ground? The sculptor will sculpt a guardian angel with the precise function of exhibiting that aspect of the greatness of God. Do we need, rather, to show how beings far superior to humankind at its highest stand in awe at the glory of God? There is an artist here who will paint the seraphim who ceaselessly acclaim it, singing the Trisagion "Holy, Holy, Holy" day and night, in celebration of that glory of the Eternal One. Has Mass become banal for us? An altarpiece will remind us that it is our banality that makes it seem so to us when in fact unseen hosts are present with us, both our own departed friends and those ubiquitous messengers of God that we call angels who, at the whisper of a prayer come scurrying to our side to help us say it better. In short, angels, far from detracting from the glory due only to God, focus our attention precisely there. And all the while, the old archetypes that lie so secure and so deep in the human psyche are left uninjured. Only their old ways of functioning and their ancient roles vanish along with their former lawlessness, now that they are turned toward the One in the service of whom "is perfect freedom." Angels in the visual arts are not merely beautiful; they provide patterns of efficiency and tireless energy in the service of the One who is "immortal, invisible, God only wise," encouraging us in the hope that one day we, who often feel so clumsy and awkward and are so easily discouraged and tired, may "put out wings like eagles" and run and "not grow weary, walk and never tire" (Isaiah 40:31, Jerusalem Bible).

11

ANGELS IN MUSIC

Sit, Jessica. Look how the floor of heaven
Is thick inlaid with patines of bright gold;
There's not the smallest orb which thou behold'st
But in his motion like an angel sings,
Still choiring to the young-eyed cherubins;
Such harmony is in immortal souls;
But whilst this muddy vesture of decay
Doth grossly close it in, we cannot hear it.

SHAKESPEARE, *The Merchant of Venice*

If the visual arts can make angels visible, surely the musical arts can make them audible. Indeed, are not angels more easily connected with music than with any other art? After all, they are so often depicted as singing or playing harps or trumpets or lutes that if we detect them at all we are surely even more likely to do so by catching the strains of their music than by imagining them in visible forms such as the painters and sculptors give them. Yet while we usually have little difficulty in recognizing an angel in the visual arts (even when it lacks wings), we do not necessarily detect them so easily in music, unless words provide us with a signal.

Suppose we begin at the most obvious place: the Christmas hymns and carols, where angel voices abound. Can we really pretend that, if we had no words to guide us, we could tell that "Hark the Herald angels sing" is about angels and that "The Holly and the Ivy" never mentions them? There is a verse in "Adeste Fideles" that any passably good choir can so sing as to make angels sweep through the clerestory and encircle the steeple with their

104

"Gloria in excelsis," but only if one knows the words or hears them. Without the words one might still have a dramatic musical effect, but could one know that one is expected to hear the angels? Why not, since in the visual arts they are so recognizable? When asked to detect their approach, I might perhaps concoct some interpretative theory about notes soaring up the scale in a crescendo only to find a more experienced listener propounding, just as convincingly, the notion that the sudden muffling of the music is the angels' cue.

The organ stop called *vox angelica* is usually four feet, while the one called *vox humana* is eight feet. The *vox angelica* is constructed in various ways but usually with free vibrating reeds and short tubes. Can this afford us a clue for the interpretation of "angelic" music? Surely it is not a very significant clue, if a clue at all. For of course the organ builders are merely following an artificial convention. There is no quality inherent in a high soprano that makes her better for "angelic" music than is a mezzo or a contralto. A boy's voice would generally be preferred to any of them because of the unique purity of its tone. The purity, not the pitch, is what counts. Then is that the determining quality in "angelic" music? Not necessarily, by any means, if angels in music behave as we have seen them behave in the visual arts where they assume all sorts of forms, male, female, and androgynous; aged and infantile. No human is so adaptable as an angel. That goes for the evil ones as well as for the good.

We began this chapter with a discussion of hymns. Hymns, however, are not a very lofty musical form. They exist for congregational purposes to help large numbers of people participate in the service liturgically. Then can we be assured of a better result if we look instead at a more musically interesting form? Suppose that someone of considerable musical discrimination and talent who knew absolutely nothing of Latin were to listen to, say, the *Laetabundus,* a medieval Christmas sequence uniquely popular in the later Middle Ages. Would he or she spot where angels are mentioned even if told to be on the lookout for them? It would seem to me most unlikely. I am sure that, were I in such a position and ignorant of Latin, I would propose several possibilities, all of them wrong, and miss the one casual angelic reference. Or think of the *Missa de Angelis,* surely an "angelic" composition if ever there were one. Would even the most musical of listeners who happened to be entirely unfamiliar with church music ever guess that it is so named, if presented with half a dozen alternative choices such as, say,

Mozart's *Coronation Mass?* I cannot see what would give such a listener as much as a hint. Even a very ordinary listener to music, such as myself, can usually discern the fall of raindrops or the swirl of autumn leaves, but could I detect the flutter of an angel's wing? Of course in music as in other expressions of the human spirit, historical knowledge is immensely helpful in directing our attention to what may be expected of us. Even in hearing a speech delivered in a language such as Finnish or Welsh that is entirely unknown to the hearer, one can often hope to discern, from a general understanding of linguistics, whether the speaker is talking of the joys of love or denouncing a political opponent or giving a weather report. At least one could make a fair guess, provided that the speaker had a reasonably civilized intonation. To that extent, then, one might hope to distinguish angels from devils and other entities in a symphony or some other sustained musical composition.

The question is discussed in some of the musicological literature, although perhaps more in connection with the bad angels than with the good ones. (So might one expect, since evil is often more alluring than good, making the Devil seem more interesting than God.) Reinhold Hammerstein, for example, in his *Diabolus in Musica,* a German study of what he calls the iconography of medieval music, focuses principally on the bad angels. One of the basic ways of alluding to them musically is through the use of what he calls *pervertierte Instrumente.* One "perverts" an instrument to produce, for instance, a horrible cacophony. When this is set beside a beautifully harmonious musical sequence, the contrast forms a pointer, along with minimal verbal help either from the title or from an advance interpretation in the published program.

Once we understand the principle behind a certain kind of music, what he calls its *metaphysisches Prinzip* (metaphysical principle), and become accustomed to the *metaphysische Polarität und Werturteil* (metaphysical polarity and value judgement), we have prepared ourselves to understand on our own the composer's language with its distinctive musical vocabulary. We are now learning to cope with a specific kind of musical "iconography," just as one learns, in the study of religion, to deal with conventional symbols within a particular religious framework such as Christianity or Mahayana Buddhism. No student of Christian art can be very long in discovering that a fish represents Jesus Christ and why it does so and that an eagle is likely to point to John as does a lion to

Mark. Nor could a student of Buddhism go far without learning to distinguish the various *mudras* or hand positions of the Buddha as iconographically represented in Buddhist art. Even when one en-counters a hitherto unknown position, one may intelligently guess at its significance through having grasped the general principle behind that type of iconography. So then in music: once we understand the general outlook behind, say, the *Faust* motif, we can begin to fill in the details.

In Schumann's *Faust,* for example, we can hear an evil angel taunting Gretschen in church. Then, in the epilogue, being trans-ported to heaven, we hear the choirs of the good angels singing. Penderecki, in his *Dies Irae,* seeks to present a hideous vision of hell on earth in which Satan and his hosts have descended to show us the nature of their terrible evil power. We hear the lamentations of the damned and the vicious shrieks of their masters. It is Auschwitz: as much a foretaste of the horrors of hell as an authentic mystical experience on earth is reckoned by some theologians to be a foretaste of the *visio beatifica,* the Vision of God that is the essence of the bliss of heaven. In this hell on earth not only is hope abandoned, just as it is by those who enter the portals of Dante's hell; the essence of the torment consists in the hopelessness even more than in the anguish and the acosmic confusion. Yet despite the misery there is a certain mournful majesty in the music, as there must be in the minds of many who behold the horror of the scene and contemplate the reality of the satanic power behind it. In medieval mythology the Devil was supposed to leave an indescrib-ably hideous stench behind him. In Penderecki's music one can almost smell his stench rising through the lamentations in this foretaste of the *poena damni* of hell: the sense of the loss of everything because the presence of God, to which we have become habituated, has been forever withdrawn.

All this is made possible, however, only by our prior understand-ing of the musical vocabulary and iconography. In Mahler's Fourth Symphony, by contrast, we hear a soprano angel singing, in an almost childlike way, a celebration of the celestial joys. (Mahler also uses angel motifs in his Second and Third Symphonies.) Massenet, in *Le Jongleur de Notre Dame,* presents moving musical imagery of the good angels carrying to heaven the soul of the humble and devout man who is a juggler by trade and has offered his juggling, all that he has, to God.

In Liszt's *Dante Symphony,* we are well prepared to hear the angelic voices in the ninth heaven to which Beatrice has wafted Dante in the twenty-seventh canto of the *Paradiso,* after he has heard St. Peter bitterly rebuking his successors in the Apostolic Chair for their avarice and power-mania while all the heavenly hosts in a celestial descant sympathetically echo the apostle's righteous indignation. (Boniface VIII, through whose wrath Dante was exiled from his beloved Florence, was indeed an impressive example of papal ambition and worldly pride.) We know to expect the circling angels ecstatically singing the praises of God. Very different is the Dance of Satan and his hosts in *Job* by Ralph Vaughan Williams, who, working in an Anglican context, was of a mystical temper and a composer whose music may perhaps be better described as religious than as pertaining to Anglican or indeed any choral church tradition.

Verdi, in his *Giovanna d'Arco,* uses a somewhat mischievous method to express the contrast between the good and the bad angels. Joan is confronted by a group of each kind. The bad ones sing what is really a variation of a Neapolitan bordello song, while the good ones sing church music. That is a comparatively simple device for a composer to use to bring home the distinction. Theologically, however, it is misleading, since it implicitly presupposes that the cause of the war between Michael and Lucifer lies in the antagonism between the spirit and the flesh. It is much more. In Christian theology the struggle of the spirit against the flesh is only a battle maneuver when seen in the context of the war itself. As Paul (or whoever is the writer of the letter to the Ephesians) puts it, the war is not only against "the flesh" but against evil spiritual powers, against "the Sovereignties and the Powers who originate the darkness in this world, the spiritual army of evil in the heavens" (Ephesians 6:12, Jerusalem Bible). True, as a senior devil reminds his apprentice in devilry in C.S. Lewis's perceptive fantasy, *The Screwtape Letters,* the fact that human beings are embodied in flesh and blood is a notable help to devils, who can turn this weakness to their advantage, exploiting it in their warfare against humanity. Nevertheless, that is merely an advantage that the evil angels have over us; it is not what the war is ultimately *about.* The real war is about a manifestation of evil that makes even the sharpest carnal temptation pale before it as a sideshow, an incidental skirmish rather than the main campaign. It is not the *casus belli,* not what the war is about in the last resort. As musical drama, however, Verdi's device is eminently successful. The contrasting imagery of the bordello and the church brings home colorfully at least one easily grasped symbol of the warfare between Lucifer and Michael, between the Devil and God. In music as in painting, color is an eloquent communicator.

"Angelic" music need not raise the question of the war between good and evil that is such a central motif in Gnostic forms of religion, Jewish, Christian, or otherwise. In Prokofiev's Third Symphony the angel who brings music to the girl is neither good nor bad; at any rate she does not seem to belong to one category or the other. Nevertheless, the entity is plainly supranatural. That is what matters here. By contrast, Wagner's *Der Engel* is a song about an angel engaged in the specific task of guiding him: a close cousin, to say the least, of the guardian angel concept, set to music.

Wherever we turn in music, then, we find that only through some understanding of the philosophical presuppositions in the composer's mind and lying far beneath the musical score can we expect to interpret the music. We must also know something about the history of music. But does all that make musical interpretation so very different from interpretation in the visual arts? It would seem that, after all, the difference cannot be a radical one. For, as we have seen, one would be no less at sea in interpreting a painting or a sculpture if one knew nothing at all of the history, the philosophy, the life-situation *(Sitz-im-Leben)* in the artist's mind. Not merely could we make nothing of the fish as a symbol of Jesus Christ in Christian art; we could make very little of the Crucifixion, while paintings of the Annunciation (that much favored subject in medieval Christian art) would be little more than pretty pictures, which critics would define only in terms of line and color combinations! Armed with a knowledge of one religious context, one might by analogy be able to understand something of the art of another (for example, a Hindu or a Buddhist one), yet not enough for adequate appreciation.

Music and dancing do have one important characteristic that separates them from the plastic arts. They have origins that go farther back in human history. They were both originally manifestations of the reproduction of sounds and of the movements of entities and phenomena in nature. Unlike even the most primitive forms of the visual arts they needed no tools other than the human voice and the human body. They played an enormous role in the life of primitive societies: in initiation ceremonies, in hunting, and in war. They were part of a network of magical ritual and intent. In developed societies they long ago lost their mimetic and magical character. Imitation is one of the most rudimentary forms of magic. Music and the dance lost their primitive, magical character before the other arts did, precisely because of their independence of instruments outside the human body. In a primitive, magic-oriented society, when one wishes to cast a spell or put a hex on anyone, it is easier and more efficient to use one's own body for the purpose than to carve a figure or paint a picture to produce the magical result. So in developed societies music and the dance lost their sacred, magical character earlier and came to acquire more quickly a profane role, allowing them to function in innumerable ways apart from any traditional place in the society's religious development. This circumstance sets them apart to some extent when it comes to interpreting their full meaning. It may be that we need to know even more history to interpret the full significance of music and dance than we do in the visual arts, because the latter are more governed by a common heritage, particularly by a religious heritage, such as Hinduism or Christianity. Nevertheless, when all that is said, the interpretation of all the arts, visual or musical, must depend on their place and function in the vast network of human history, no less than on the philosophical presuppositions in the minds of the artists and composers. We must know, therefore, how angels function in the minds of these artists and composers if we are to pretend to understand and appreciate their function in the works and performances in which they appear.

12

ANGEL-LIKE BEINGS IN OTHER RELIGIONS

Will there be any beings in the future period . . . who when these words of the Sutra are being taught, will understand their truth?— The Lord replied: Do not speak thus, Subhuti! Yes, even then there will be such beings. For even at that time, Subhuti, there will be Bodhisattvas who are gifted with good conduct, gifted with virtuous qualities, gifted with wisdom, and who . . . will understand their truth. And these Bodhisattvas, Subhuti, will not be such as have honoured only one single Buddha. . . . On the contrary . . . they will be such as have honoured many hundreds of thousands of Buddhas. . . .

Diamond Sutra

Now that we have considered angels as they have appeared historically within the Judaeo-Christian tradition (which is also the heritage of Islam), we must ask: whence came the concept of angels? Did the biblical authors have any prototypes to work from in the history of ideas? Are there counterparts to angels in other religions, such as Theravada and Mahayana Buddhism, that have a different historical background and in which, therefore, such counterparts might be expected to have functions that differ, at least in some respects, from those of angels in the three great religions (Judaism, Christianity, and Islam) that share a common Semitic heritage? To deal with such questions we need first to glance at some historical background.

India is a land of incalculable antiquity to which, during some centuries about 3,500 years ago a people of Indo-European stock

111

who called themselves Aryans (the word means "noble" or "lord") came pouring in across the Hindu Kush mountain passes, eventually conquering the inhabitants of India and remaking that great subcontinent. They belonged to a complex group which also migrated in several other directions, bringing their language as well as their blood into the peoples that we now call Greeks, Latins, Germans, Celts, and Slavs. Another branch of this complex ethnic group, whom historians now call Indo-Aryan, moved into Iran. Although the religious development of India and Iran was eventually to proceed on very different lines (what we call Hinduism and Zoroastrianism are strikingly different), the ancient, pre-Zoroastrian religion of Iran and the religion of India in the early Vedic period[1] had some common features.

One of these is the use of the word *deva* or *daeva* for the gods. In the *Rig-Veda* the Sanskrit term *deva* is used habitually for the gods, some of whom may be identified with ancient Iranian counterparts, for example, the Iranian Intar (or Indara) with Indra (one of the greatest among the Indian deities) and Mithra with the Vedic Mitra. The word *deva* is taken to mean "shining one" and from it comes, of course, the Latin word *deus*. Through the linguistic affinities among languages of Indo-Aryan origin we can see clear relations between one religious idea and another and could do so to a remarkable extent even in the absence of other historical knowledge. For example, the affinity between the Sanskrit *Dyaush-Pitar,* the sky god, and the Greek *Zeus Pater,* who came to preside over the Greek pantheon, is well known to linguists and fairly obvious. Devas, in one form or another, constituted the pantheon of any polytheistic society with Indo-Aryan roots. They were arranged in some sort of hierarchical order: necessarily so, for in a polytheistic culture the pantheon includes, alongside deities of primary national importance and those ruling basic human concerns such as love and war, others of comparatively trivial or transitory significance.

The Hebrews, after the Babylonian Exile, were much influenced by the religious ideas they encountered among their captors. Although the precise extent of Iranian and other influences on the biblical writers is controversial, its importance is beyond dispute. The devas were among the imports, but before they could be naturalized in a society that had developed along such strongly monotheistic lines, they had to undergo adaptation. As the first of the Ten Commandments makes clear, there could be "no other gods before" Yahweh; nevertheless, there could be subordinate agents to attend him and to do his bidding when suitably invested with ambassadorial or other powers. By the time of Ezekiel, Yahweh had become so lofty and remote that he could be approached only through intermediaries. Angels, patterned after the old devas but adapted to the monotheistic system, functioned as such. The Hebrews were already prepared for the idea of angels as divine messengers, but now they could have a new role as heavenly courtiers around the divine throne, arranged in hierarchical order, somewhat as nobles are arranged in descending ranks from duke to baron under British and other systems. The old belief in demons or evil spirits was similarly developed into an organization with Satan as its head.

I have mentioned Iran (Persia) as among influences that probably affected the development of biblical ideas after the Babylonian Exile. Zoroaster, pre-eminent among the religious influences in Iranian history, taught a strict monotheism. The date of his birth is highly controversial, with scholarly estimates varying between about 630 BCE to as early as 1000 BCE, although the truth is probably much nearer the former date than the latter. Before his appearance the Iranian religion seems to have been somewhat similar to that of India in the Vedic period, including fire worship, which is of interest since fire plays a part in the ceremonies of Zoroastrian worship down to the present day. Zoroaster, who (even discounting many of the stories about him as legendary) must have been one of the greatest figures in the religious history of humankind, sought to wean his people away from their old polytheistic attitudes and practices and lead them toward an ethical monotheism that was very much like that expounded by the great Hebrew prophets. He wished them to worship only Ahura Mazda, the Supreme One, the All-wise, the Pure Light. He recognized, nevertheless, that Ahura Mazda, although supreme, is not unopposed. Against him is the Evil Spirit (Angra Mainyu), called in later times Shaitin (Satan). As the great Persian Empire was spreading, moving into Egypt and toward Europe, the original monotheistic strictness was modified in the sense that the old Aryan nature gods slid back (if surreptitiously and in disguise) into popular religion. They are distinctly Aryan in character with recognizably Aryan names: plainly a harking back to the archetypes from which Zoroaster had sought to emancipate his people. Among them are angels *(Yazatas)* who seem to tower above all other devas. Sometimes forty of them are named, but we also hear of them in thousands. Of course other great changes have taken place in Zoroastrianism throughout the ages. After the meteoric speed of Muslim expansion, many Zoroastrians resolved to leave their native land and migrate southward, ending in India where, in the tolerant spirit of Hinduism, they came to be recognized as the Parsees (Persians), where they prospered as a respected segment in the great mix of cultures in India. The history of this great religion shows us once again that devas do not readily die. Even among the Zoroastrians, with their traditional emphasis on Zoroaster's principle of the supremacy of the One God, they reappeared as angels. As we shall see later in this chapter, angels play a most important role in Islam, a religion in which monotheism is so emphasized as to be expressed with what strikes many non-Muslims as baneful repetitiousness.

Devas, as they appear in Buddhist thought, are beings who inhabit a heavenly sphere not accessible to or even visible to mortals. They are not themselves, however, immortal in the sense in which the leading gods in a pantheon are generally assumed to be immortal. They are subject, for instance, to the law of reincarnation under the karmic principle. They have evil counterparts, the *asuras* (compare this word with the Iranian *ahura,* which is, however, a good spirit), who engage in constant warfare against the devas. They too are subject to the law of rebirth. Nevertheless, in contrast to the *devas* they are relatively low in the hierarchy of being.

From all this we can conclude that, whatever else devas and angels may be, they represent what we see as an ideal for ourselves. That is not to say that one consciously yearns to be an angel; on the contrary, the thought of it may alarm one, but if so, it is either because one does not feel ready for such a leap or because one does not believe the leap can be made. It is perhaps conceivable that "Lucy,"[2] three million years ago, might have seen a vision of a woman grander in the scale of being than herself, but it is all but inconceivable that she could have harbored any yearning to become one. Perhaps, however, some ancestor nearer to *homo sapiens* might have cherished, however dimly, such an ambition. In the same way, I might very well see angels as what humanity may become, without feeling entirely ready to accept an invitation to be promoted overnight to their status.

One of the noblest and most endearing concepts in both Theravada and Mahayana Buddhism is that of the bodhisattva. The doctrines of reincarnation and karma, which the Buddha inherited from his native Hinduism are doctrines of spiritual evolution. The evolutionary aim is the attainment of *bodhi* (enlightenment). The Sanskrit term *bodhisattva* (in Pali, *bodhisatta)* was used at first of one who was accounted a future Buddha. It was used of Gotama himself in designating his state before his enlightenment. In Mahayana Buddhism, however, the term came to have new meaning and enhanced importance. It was contended that the old ideal was self-enlightenment, while the new one transcended that, putting compassion on an equal footing with enlightenment as the sought-after goal.

Although the process of becoming a bodhisattva may be long and arduous, caste does not enter into it, since Buddhism from the first renounced the Hindu caste system. So anyone can become a bodhisattva. According to the teaching of Nāgārjuna in the first century CE, one becomes a bodhisattva when one has reached a point at which one's mind can no more revert to its unenlightened state, being no longer capable of repudiating its noble destiny. The bodhisattva is, in this view, poised between heaven and earth. His destiny is assured. He can be reborn under the karmic principle but he will not be born into a miserable condition, such as that of a poor and ignorant family. He will be distinguished for his compassion no less than for his wisdom. Great teachers and royal personages, insofar as their efforts are directed to the love and service of others, could be bodhisattvas. What characterizes the bodhisattva above all is total altruism. He understands the interrelatedness of all things; his compassion is a consequence of this understanding.

There are, however, various ways in which the bodhisattva is understood in the multifaceted panorama of Buddhist traditions. The Theravada scriptures allude to the bodhisattva as a very rare phenomenon, while in popular Mahayana bodhisattvas are innumerable. They are enthroned in heaven, but their eyes gaze down in compassion at the world we live in and they descend to minister to us as needed. They are indeed angels of mercy.

Buddhist teaching generally does not confine bodhisattvas to Buddhism. Theoretically, to say the least, anyone may become a bodhisattva: a Muslim, for example. Indeed, even someone who classifies himself as an atheist or non-believer in religion at large might very well be a bodhisattva in the making. Anyone who is predominantly serving humanity rather than himself might be a candidate. Mother Teresa would certainly be qualified, or anyone else whose energy is predominantly spent in the service of others. The Dalai Lama, in an interview conducted by William Buckley, emphasized this aspect of Theravada Buddhism of which he is as official an exponent as one is likely to encounter.

In the Mahayana of China and Japan is to be found more especially the singularly beautiful concept of the bodhisattva as one who is ready for buddhahood but chooses to dally, temporarily renouncing that completion of his glorious destiny in order that he may stay behind to help us. Such bodhisattvas are therefore in many ways (despite obvious theological, cultural, and historical differences) clear counterparts to angels in the Judaeo-Christian tradition. A notable difference, however, is that they have arisen from and transcended human bondage, while biblical angels, like the devas of the polytheistic religions, are generally supposed to belong to a radically different order of existence.

Islam, youngest of the great religions of the world, has a notably different history from that of Hinduism and Buddhism and a very different spirit, to say the least. The Arabs whom Muhammad unified under the banner of Islam had developed various cultic practices, but the majority had recognized tribal gods and goddesses, mostly counterparts to the deities familiar in polytheistic societies everywhere. Mecca itself was the center of a phallic cult associated with three goddesses especially venerated there. There were also other, lesser spirits: the *jinn,* of whom we read in the famous stories collected under the title *The Thousand and One Nights,* more commonly known as *The Arabian Nights.* These jinn might be friendly or hostile, somewhat like the elves and fairies of other cultures. Many superstitious fears and hopes were associated with belief in these spirits. Angels were also known and seem all to have been beneficent toward humankind, but they seem also to have played a lesser part in the imaginations of the people. They were probably imports from monotheistic sources (Judaism and Zoroastrianism) taken out of context and added to the pantheon. Polytheistic religions have an infinite capacity for incorporating anything in the way of such supernatural entities.

When Muhammad established his uncompromisingly monotheistic faith, he recognized prophets, including Moses and Jesus among them. He also, however, took account of angels. They were already known entities and were part of the biblical scenario from which he took much of the material he used in the construction of his new religion. On the "Night of Power and Glory" it was Gabriel who addressed Muhammad. As we have seen earlier, the Qur'ān teaches that the angels, having been created before man, were summoned by Allah to bow down before man, his latest and greatest creation. Satan and others refused and fell accordingly. The good angels' primary function is to praise God and serve him; but angels play a definite part in the Muslim faith, for instance as witnesses for or against man on the Day of Judgment. Recording angels are present at prayer in the mosque and elsewhere. The Qur'ān also recognizes jinn. These are in some ways more like human beings than angels are, but of a different "substance." As in pre-Islamic Arabian religion they may be good or bad. The latter kind serve Satan who, according to Islamic teaching, will have authority over all whom he has captured for his side in his rebellion against Allah.

The jinn of pre-Islamic lore in the Arab world, who survived to the point of having some degree of recognition in the Qur'ān, have counterparts in almost all societies. From Scandinavia to Iran, from Ireland to South America, popular folklore is full of allusions to such elemental spirits as imps, elves, pixies, gnomes, banshees, gremlins, goblins, pucks, trolls, leprechauns, peris, kobolds, and other "little people" who have been carried over from old Celtic, Scandinavian, Teutonic, or other old folklore.

When Christianity became *religio licita* under Constantine in the early fourth century, eventually acquiring the status of an establishment of sorts, it obviously could not tolerate the continued recognition of the greater figures of the old pantheon: the gods and goddesses of the polytheistic religions it gradually displaced. The displacement was indeed very gradual. The "death of the gods" was slow, especially in Scandinavia, which was not christianized till more than a thousand years after the death of Christ. Even in the southern regions of Europe, however, people clung to the old "pagan" gods, particularly in the less populated areas. (The word "pagan" meant "country fellow.") In the long run, however, the old deities had to go. The Christian Church could find no place for, nor could it tolerate talk of, the old gods of war and love, of fertility and harvest. To some extent devotion to the saints was psychologically a substitute and could flourish within a strict biblical monotheism such as the Church expounded.

Santa Claus was an exception. Unashamedly an old pagan god of some consequence he managed to survive in popular lore, perhaps because, being so obviously of pagan origin and in any case a jovial figure, he could pose no threat to Christian faith.

Something like this sort of toleration was extended on a larger scale to the little sprites of ancient popular belief. Being neither gods nor goddesses, not even angels or demons, not even devas or bodhisattvas, the Church could gracefully wink at them in the expectation of their eventual demise. They are still, however, very much alive in popular superstition, not least in countries and regions within the Celtic heritage.

Who are they and how, according to such popular belief, do they function? They are not powerful and malevolent spirits such as Satan and his minions and they certainly are not emissaries of the One True God as are the biblical angels. They are, rather, playful little agencies, often childishly mischievous and irresponsible. They "make things go bump in the night." They misplace or mislay small objects which they deftly remove out of sheer mischief, merrily (or as we sometimes say "puckishly") grinning with amusement at us. Their disposition seems to vary from individual to individual: folklore always presupposes "good fairies" and "bad fairies"; but in general they are better described as wanton, irrational, mischievous little spirits. Nevertheless, Christian teaching would have us invoke the saying attributed to Jesus: "He that is not with me is against me; and he that gathereth not with me scattereth abroad" (Matthew 12:30). Such sprites, then, would have to be ranged on the side of the evil agencies, even although they are too irresponsible for Satan to enlist them as reliable forces in his infernal army. At any rate, they are to be sharply distinguished from angels, both from angels in the service of God and from those others whom we have called "angels gone wrong."

Angels or their counterparts (such as devas and bodhisattvas) have an important function both in the strictly monotheistic and in the non-monotheistic religions of the world. They seem to be indispensable wherever men and women take seriously the existence of any dimension of being beyond a positivistic one. Whether they are regarded as a separate creation of God, or as a more advanced stage in the evolutionary process, or again (as some theosophists might prefer to say) as belonging to a different line of evolutionary development, they represent a religious idea far too significant to be ignored or treated with the mild amusement generally extended to elves and pixies. They persist in even the most highly developed religions of the world. Could they really exist? If so, how could we understand them in the light of what we know about the universe?

Now that we have considered so many aspects of the history of the concept of angels, it is time to apply ourselves to another and very different task: to consider (1) whether we are to take the concept of angels as a merely fanciful but picturesque notion in the human psyche or to regard it seriously as representing ontological realities and, if so, (2) how, in the light of what we know through modern philosophy and science, we can possibly fit them, however speculatively, into the contemporary scenario.

PART II

ANGELS
AS AN
EVOLUTIONARY
POSSIBILITY

13

ARE ANGELS MERE FICTIONS OF THE RELIGIOUS IMAGINATION?

> The result is that the super-ego of the child is not really built up on the model of the parents, but on that of the parents' super-ego; it takes over the same content, it becomes the vehicle of tradition and of all the age-long values which have been handed down in this way from generation to generation.
>
> FREUD, *New Introductory Lectures on Psychoanalysis,* "The Anatomy of the Mental Personality"

Everyone who has seriously studied religion recognizes that we all, in one way or another, make God in our own image. A German is supposed to have said that an Englishman's idea of God is an Englishman twelve feet tall. In some forms of iconography God is represented as an old man with a beard. Xenophanes of Ionia remarked thousands of years ago that if horses could draw pictures they might draw God as a splendid horse. Even when we get away from crude anthropomorphic representations of God, however, we still use symbols which, however elegant and sophisticated we may account them, are still only symbols. We think about everything in symbolic form. The teacher who was able to get through to Helen Keller, despite her pupil's enormous handicaps, was able to do so by means of symbols adapted to her condition, beginning with the experience and the concept of water. The chemist uses a much more streamlined symbol (H_2O), but it is nonetheless, of course, only a symbol. It is not surprising, then, that we need and use symbols in talking of

123

religious experience and ideas associated with it, such as the idea of God.

The question remains, however: do these religious symbols stand for a reality outside us or do they merely describe an experience within us that we project? Specifically, although few of us really suppose that angels exist in human form, clothed in white robes and winged like swans, the difficulty does not end there. To put the question more bluntly, do angels, whatever they are, really have an independent existence or are they, as are Santa Claus's helpers, mere poetic conceits, concocted by human imagination to help to express the ideas of generosity and gift-giving that are associated with what we vaguely call "the Spirit of Christmas"?

First of all we ought to notice that once we recognize that Santa's helpers are mere figments of the human imagination we are well on the way to recognizing that so also is Santa Claus himself. We know, as a matter of historical fact, that Santa Claus is a hangover from an old pagan deity who, like much else in the European pagan background of Christianity, was only very superficially christened. Indeed, in some representations he has even been given a little cross on his helmet to disguise his otherwise somewhat obvious origin in the pagan lore of Wodan and the Valkyries. Why should not what is true of Santa and his helpers also be true of God and the angels?

When human beings think and talk of God and the angels are they not only representing but also creating these beings? The view that the roots of religion lie solely in human needs is familiar to all who have read Freud. It is, however, a much more ancient view. Demosthenes, some three and a half centuries before Christ, observed: "What a man wishes, that he believes to be true."[1] The Epicurean school of philosophy taught, centuries before Christ, that most human ills are attributable to religion, which has its origin in fear, a view expressed by Lucretius[2] and later by the Roman poet Statius.[3] In the nineteenth century, Ludwig Feuerbach (1804–1872), who directly influenced Karl Marx, treated all objects of religious attention as imaginative creations of men and women in the expression of their subjective longings. He called them *personifizierte Wünsche,* personified wishes. Religion, then, is a human dream. A dream is not nothing and does not deal with nothing, but the dreamer sees real things "in the entrancing splendor of imagination and caprice instead of in the simple daylight of reality and necessity." The religious person lifts the object of his dreams and transposes it to reality.[4] Feuerbach, most of whose work was done before the publication of Darwin's *Origin of Species,* could talk of man's essential nature, because people then could still think of humanity as a species distinct from all others and having a special, fixed nature of its own. By contrast we must nowadays see humanity as a process rather than a species.

The view that religious concepts such as God and the angels are in fact only the creations of our mind and therefore to be dealt with in purely psychological terms is nevertheless one that must be taken seriously. As we have seen, it is, in one form or another, of great antiquity. It also seems, at least at first sight, to be very plausible. We all recognize that the gods of the ancient polytheisms were projections of the human mind. No educated person in any developed country today would claim to believe in, say, Venus or Mars. We would simply recognize such gods and goddesses as part of the ancient mythologies. But then, it is difficult to say to what extent and in what way intelligent people even in ancient Greece or Rome would have said that they believed in such deities. Socrates certainly did not; indeed he was charged with openly repudiating belief in them. Nevertheless, Venus, the goddess of love, does indeed stand for a most important reality in my life: the reality of sex, with all its troubles and joys. True, it is within me and is part of me, giving rise to longings and fantasies to which I may give this or that expression; but it assuredly lies beyond me too. It is, to say the least, an important aspect of biological existence and, although human sexuality has very distinctive features that give it a poignancy and a complexity not found in the lower forms of mammalian life, I am aware of sexuality as a very formidable reality in the whole biological spectrum. War, likewise, is unfortunately characteristic of all life. We see of course the need to do all we can to control it and think that civilized societies ought to be able to eliminate it. It still persists, alas, as a very great reality in our lives. We need hardly be reminded that it could even bring about our annihilation. So Mars, the symbolic personification of war, cannot be said to be a mere construct of my mind; he is, on the contrary, one of the great realities of my experience, however inadequately he may be symbolically represented in conventional statuary.

The question then is: what *kind* of realities are represented by personifications such as Mars and Venus? They are surely realities that permeate all life. If, through some nuclear catastrophe, for example, all life on our planet were totally destroyed, then presumably the realities we designate as Venus and Mars would be destroyed with it. Can we say, then, that whatever it is that the Bible calls God would be destroyed too? Not at all, if by "God" we refer to a principle (however much more besides) that is at the heart of the universe as its ground and its source. If we are wrong in supposing that there is any such ground or source, then of course our use of the term "God" will need much modification. That will not mean, however, that it will become a term with no referent outside our own imaginings.

The fact that an idea grows within my imagination and is ordered and constructed by me according to my own limited capacity does not mean that it has no meaning beyond me, or that it has no meaning beyond the human race to which I belong. *All* our ideas are developed in our own minds and (as thoughtful people have known for centuries) transformed in the course of our mental processing of them. We cannot suppose that even the most ordinary perceptions that we have of the world around us correspond to the state of affairs that we represent to ourselves in these perceptions. Sunsets please me; roaches displease me; but neither can be pleasing or displeasing in itself, with no one to be pleased or displeased by them. In perceiving the sun as I do at sunrise, at sunset, or at noonday, I believe I am in some way perceiving a reality, but much of my perception is put there by myself. It looks to me as though the sun were falling into or rising out of the ocean, but I know that it is not really so. All this is commonplace in the history of philosophy. It should not obscure for us the fact that ideas do not grow in my mind by spontaneous generation. They originate beyond me, whatever I do to them when I get them.

Freud's hypothesis of the superego was an attempt within the framework of his psychoanalytical system to explain our human striving for what are commonly called "the higher things of life." The superego in the psyche, he points out, is not built merely of the restraining moral injunctions of one's parents but includes also one's parents' parents and so on back through a tradition of age-long values; the superego is the vehicle of their transmission. When, inevitably, we ask why the ego should be willing to submit so often and so abjectly to this even more mysterious part of the Freudian psyche, Freud is at pains to establish the reality of the superego as a psychological entity. He tells us that in 1921 he tried to apply the distinction between ego and superego to the study of group psychology. He reached a formula of the following sort: a person representing a moral authority or ethical ideal is adopted by various individuals who become a group and recognize one another as belonging to that group; the image of this person can then act as the superego for the whole group. The function of the superego is repressive. That is its essential nature. Even, for example, in face of an overpowering sexual urge, the superego may assert its authority so decisively as to inhibit the satisfaction of the urge as effectively as if it were a Victorian schoolmaster armed with a flexible cane.

Now of course the Freudian geography of the psyche divided into ego, superego, and id is a persuasive way of describing what we all recognize (and what people for thousands of years before Freud recognized) about the human condition. It takes into account, moreover, the irrationality of some of the phobias that have been somehow instilled into us by a parent who in turn has had them instilled into him or into her in similarly irrational ways. One may be programmed in such a way to fear, say, red-haired people, which would be of course quite irrational. But are all injunctions from such quarters of my psyche equally lacking in foundation? Is my horror of cannibalism, for instance, and the shudder that I feel at the notion of an entrée of human flesh as unfounded as, say, a distaste for redheads? True though it is that man has an apparently limitless capacity for self-deception, does it follow that the entire evolution of the moral sentiments of humankind over thousands of years has been no more than a tediously prolonged exhibition of that human weakness? Surely not, and if not, whence comes the force that has improved not only man's intellectual range but refined his moral awareness? Has he spun it around him as the larva spins a cocoon around itself before entering the pupa stage of its metamorphosis? If I feel liberated in overcoming a dislike of redheads that has been genetically or otherwise programmed into me, am I then to proceed to demolish the rest of my inherited psychological prejudices and return to a healthier state in which I can sit down comfortably to enjoy a cannibalistic feast?

Of course not. The superego, like all such psychic constructs, is no more than a psychic receptacle or receiving set in the use of which I must learn to acquire powers of discrimination, as one may find out how to discern, amid the bulk of televised trash, some programs of rare value of one sort or another. We ask, then, what is the magnet that attracts the human psyche "upward" and that is so feebly and sometimes so inefficiently reflected in the working of that aspect of it that Freud chose to call the superego? Theists will readily answer that of course it is God, which is a neat answer indeed; but we may well find more immediately useful the concept of various dimensions of existence through which we are passing on our long evolutionary journey that slowly leads those of us who are willing to listen to the "angel voices" more and more into enhanced awareness of a higher dimension that is already impinging upon us.

Jung, as is well known, had a much greater interest in religious symbolism than had Freud. His interest apparently sprang from the fact that in his clinical work he had come to find that the methods of Freud and of Adler, although they worked well with patients under thirty-five, were inadequate in dealing with the problems of patients over that age. He tells us that among the latter class he never once found a patient "whose problem in the last resort was not that of finding a religious outlook on life. It is safe to say that every one of them fell ill because he had lost that which the living religions of every age have given to their followers, and none of them has been really healed who did not regain his religious outlook."[5] Nevertheless, Jung's focus was always on the psychological aspect of religion; that is, he eschewed, at least professionally, the discussion of the ontological questions that all highly developed religions pose: questions about the reality of the religious object *beyond* the psychological phenomenon. God is treated, therefore, simply as "a function of the unconscious, namely, the manifestation of a split-off sum of libido, which has activated the *God-imago.*"[6]

So when he speaks of angels, as he does to a considerable extent, it is always within that psychological framework of his theory of the *psyche.* So he sees birds, for example, as symbolizing spirits and angels.[7] They symbolize mythological births. He associates them with "the rebirth of the phoenix" and remarks: "Divine messengers frequently appear at these mythological births, as can be seen from the use we still make of *god-parents.*"[8] Presumably (although I have not noticed an explicit reference in Jung's writings) the stork who, according to an age-old legend, brings the newborn child from the sky, is an angelic messenger from God.

Jung also refers to the passage in Genesis (Genesis 6:2) that relates that "the sons of God saw the daughters of men, that they were fair; and they took them wives of all of which they chose." He tells us that Byron's unfinished poem, *Heaven and Earth,* is founded on that passage and that he chose as a motto for it words from Coleridge, "And woman waiting for her demon-lover." "The angels Samiasa and Azaziel burn with sinful love for the beautiful daughters of Cain, Anah and Aholibamah, and thus break through the barrier between mortals and immortals. Like Lucifer, they rebel against God. . . . If we translate this projection back into the psychological sphere from whence it came, it would mean that the good and rational Power which rules the world with wise laws is threatened by the chaotic, primitive force of passion. . . . As a power which transcends consciousness the libido is by nature daemonic: it is both God and the Devil. If evil were to be utterly destroyed, everything daemonic, including God himself, would suffer a grievous loss; it would be like performing an amputation on the body of the Deity." A little later Jung continues: "Man continues to be man. Through excess of longing he can draw the gods down into the murk of his passion. He seems to be raising himself up to the Divine, but in doing so he abandons his humanity. Thus the love of Anah and Aholibamah for their angels becomes the ruin of gods and men."[9] In another place Jung recounts the curious Jewish legend that Adam, before he knew Eve, had another wife called Lilith: a demon-wife, with whom he strove for supremacy. Lilith rose up in the air and Adam forced her to return to him, in which he used the help of three angels.[10] Here Jung again sees the motif of the "helpful bird" for "angels are really birds." He reminds us that in "the Mithraic sacrifice the messenger of the gods—'the angel'—was a raven; the messenger is winged (Hermes). In Jewish tradition angels are masculine. The symbolism of the angels is important because it signifies the upper, aerial, spiritual triad in conflict with the *one,* lower, feminine power."[11]

As might be expected of Jung, angels for him are simply part of an elaborate system of symbolism reflective of the labyrinthine odysseys of the human psyche. He treats Nietzsche, whose thought much influenced his own, in much the same way. Such treatment tells us a great deal about Jung's theory of the psyche, some of which we may find persuasive in its way, but really nothing about angels or supermen as ontological possibilities. Dragons and swans may equally play a role in the meanderings of the psyche, but the fact that one is fictitious and the other a well-known ornithological entity is irrelevant to Jung's concerns.

This brief excursus into the psychology of religion should have shown us at least one important fact. Freudian, Jungian, or other theories about the psychology of religion may or may not seem plausible in their treatment of psychological aspects of religious phenomena. Their danger lies in the fact that many people take them to be studies of religion. They are no more studies of religion than studies in the psychology of bird-watching are studies of bird-watching. Everything that we humans think or say or do has a psychological aspect and everything that we do societally has a sociological aspect. When we are studying the psychology of art or the psychology of business or the psychology of language, we must be careful not to suppose that we are thereby studying art or business or language. We may be studying some questions that have a bearing on some aspects of the study of art, business, and language; but we most certainly are not exhausting the study of these fields if indeed we are even thereby beginning it. The importance of this distinction and the danger of psychologism cannot easily be exaggerated.

If we are to take seriously our study of angels (and I can see little point in studying them at all unless we study them seriously), we must make the distinction upon which I have just been insisting. It may be interesting to notice that some mathematicians, when they solve a difficult equation, jump up in the air with joy while others of a less excitable temperament merely breathe a little more freely or even do nothing observable at all; but whatever conclusions may be drawn from such observations, they tell us nothing at all about mathematics. It is of paramount importance to recognize that much the same is true of studies in the psychology of religion. What psychologists and psychoanalysts say about what they plausibly theorize from clinical experience to be how angels function in the human psyche tells us nothing one way or the other about angels.

We can now better address ourselves to the central question raised in this chapter: are angels mere fictions of the religious imagination? Yes and no. In one sense of course they are fictions, as indeed is everything else in our conceptual processes. Whether we see them as winged and haloed youths or as the "separated intelligences" of learned medieval thought, we are clothing whatever reality they have in the habiliments necessary to make them intelligible in our eyes.

Perhaps, however, we prefer to say something like this: if it has taken us so long to reach the intellectual and spiritual level that makes possible our attainment of a recognizably human condition and if at the same time we see both the ludicrously limited character of that condition and the unlimited possibilities it seems to contain, surely there must be beings somewhere who have evolved beyond even the best of us. That, however, might take us only as far as any intelligent and imaginative schoolchild might go in feeling sure that there must be planets somewhere, perhaps far away in one of the outer galaxies, on which flourish a race of beings superior in intelligence to us.

But suppose that we have already accepted the view, proclaimed in the biblical documents, that the entire universe depends on a Being who not only creates and sustains it but whose concern extends to even the falling of a sparrow. Then, in the light of what we know about evolution, we shall need little further thought to accept the view that this Being, having surely created higher forms of life and intelligence than ourselves, will employ some such higher agencies to guide and help us in our struggles along the evolutionary path. Moreover, anyone who is sufficiently aware of the reality and importance of a spiritual dimension of being to permit him or her to acknowledge the reality of the biblical God must surely be already attuned to the presence of invisible "ministers of grace" in such a way that accepting the biblical representation of them as angels will in no way offend his or her mind.

14

FROM HOMINIDS TO SUPRAHUMANS

Lucy: a lady three million years old.

Now that we have surveyed the history of the role of angels in biblical and other classical documents of Christian thought and practice and have explored patristic and medieval attitudes with some reference to their ideological roots, we inevitably ask: is it possible for us to take angels seriously today, in the light of modern knowledge and in the context of our contemporary understanding of how things work in the universe? Must we dismiss them, perhaps with a wistful nod and a nostalgic smile as ancient archetypes that have ceased to have meaning for us as ontological realities, or is there any way in which we can find an intelligible place for them?

To succeed in doing so would not mean that we had "proved" their existence. Few philosophically-trained theologians today would claim the possibility of "proving" the existence of God, preferring to insist, rather, that an idea so vigorously attested by faith and at the same time philosophically viable ought to be taken very seriously indeed by all educated and intelligent people.

As was stated in the Introduction, the universe must be understood in evolutionary terms. Is it then possible that angels might have an intelligible place and function within an evolutionary

132

framework? To establish a background for exploring this possibility let us look first at how humanity as we know it has already evolved. From that, we can learn at least *one aspect* of that all-pervasive, universal principle.

We know more and more about our hominid ancestors, who were bipedal for several million years. An international team led by Dr. Donald Johanson discovered, at Hadar, Ethiopia, in 1974, a partial skeleton, identified as an adult female of about twenty-five. The discovery was made at a stratum about three million years old. She was nicknamed Lucy. Other similar finds have been made in other parts of the world. Lucy and others of her age and species are the oldest form of hominids that anthropologists have discovered. They are named *Australopithecus afarensis*. Lucy's jaws were apelike and she probably had very strong limbs. She was quite short (about forty-four inches) and probably weighed only about sixty-five pounds. More significantly, her brain is likely to have been only about a third of the size of the average human brain today. Other hominids appeared later, such as *Australopithecus boisei* and *Homo habilis*. Eventually the larger-brained *Homo erectus* appeared and flourished for more than a million years. Then primitive forms of *Homo sapiens* began to appear about 300,000 years ago.

What a staggeringly long stretch of time it has taken to move from such hominids to what we recognize today as "the human race"! Yet the differences in Lucy's physical appearance and ours, great though they are, are as nothing compared to the difference in brain size and therefore in mental development. If we think of the process in theological terms with God as the creative source behind that development within man and even his more immediate ancestors, we must concur in the ancient Greek saying that the mills of God grind slow but sure.

Unless, however, we live at an exceptionally low level of awareness, we must surely ponder, at least from time to time, what lies ahead. We now know a good deal about whence we came in the evolutionary process; but whither are we bound? Lucy must have lived in what we can only call another dimension of existence from ours: not *wholly* different, of course; not even a dog's or a cat's is wholly different; but the dimension in which she would have lived out her life must have been very restricted compared with that of even comparatively unadvanced human beings in today's world. May there be other dimensions of existence superior to ours? Can we really be sure that, in all the unimaginably immense universe, we are the best there is? Perhaps on another planet in another galaxy there exist more advanced forms of life than ours. May it even be that a dimension of existence lies far nearer to us, invisible and intangible to the senses we habitually use?

When we talk of another dimension of being, what precisely do we mean? A realm of angels and demons, of spirits and the like, may seem weird to many of us. Notoriously such notions are susceptible to outrageous abuse by charlatans and frauds; yet in one form or another they are part of the very stuff of all authentic religious experience. The Bible, for instance, is full of them. Are they mere figments of fancy?

According to Gallup polls and other such statistical analyses, the vast majority of people in America and a large preponderance elsewhere, although they may have no church affiliation at all and want none, acknowledge a firm belief in God. What then of that other dimension of being through which, according to the teaching of most religions, divine help comes to us, mediated in one way or another? Is not such a belief bound up with belief in God and, if so, ought not we to take it more seriously than many of us do? I find indeed that the churchless are often more open to such enquiry than are many churchfolk. Ought not all believers to be profoundly concerned with the possibility of that other dimension of existence that so many find impinging upon their daily lives, belief in which is traditionally fundamental in the major religions of the world, not least in Christianity?

We live habitually in a dimension in which our human consciousness is attuned to the empirical world to which the five senses introduce us. We are programmed by what so enters our brains. Our brains reflect on what they receive in this way. This aspect of our intellectual capacity and activity, highly complex though it is, does not radically differ from that of a computer. Our brains do indubitably function as computers, assembling and arranging the information provided to them and furnishing us with the results at such amazing speed that we are not normally aware that such an immensely complex computer-process has taken place at all.

In contrast to the brains of dogs and cats, even the most undeveloped of human brains is capable of an immensely enhanced range of capacities. Clever as my dog may be in his canine way, he cannot ever do what even a dull little boy or girl does routinely at grade school. Relying on his remarkable instincts, he may sometimes astonish me with his powers of memory, but these powers are not only extremely limited compared with even the most commonplace human ones; they are of a different order. He may learn to do and to remember how to do tricks that qualify him to perform in a circus; he may find his way home from a hundred miles away; but to expect him to acquire, say, the capacity to relate the date of Lincoln's assassination to that of the birth of Washington in any sort of historical perspective would be as ludicrous as expecting a horse to compose a sonnet.

Moreover, he has no means of appreciating the nature or the scope of even the most pedestrian of our human proclivities. He may perceive in some way the results of our superior order of mental skills. He may sometimes even stand in awe or fear of their results, but he can no more emulate their attainment than he could hope to fly like a sparrow. We, for our part, may feel a protective duty toward him: a sort of *noblesse oblige*. He can outrun me any day and hear sounds beyond the range of my hearing; but he is simply not in my league when it comes to even the most ordinary mental operations in which humans engage even in early childhood.

The difference between us and the lower mammals, even dolphins and simians, is obvious enough; but the difference between the least and the most highly developed of humans, although much less plainly discernible to the senses, is also stupendous. In undeveloped societies people may get along very well with a vocabulary of two hundred words or fewer and their entire life may have to be focused almost exclusively on the immediate needs of the body: obtaining food, maintaining warmth, and fulfilling the sexual and other urges we share with other mammals. This was no doubt to some extent true of the patriarchal society depicted in those parts of the Bible that relate to the earlier history of the Hebrew people. For despite the remarkable insights their prophets and other seers were able to attain, even the prophetic leaders of the earlier period of Hebrew history engaged in little if any philosophical or theological reflection. By and large they were too busy eking out a living on the edge of the death-dealing desert and defending themselves against the military might of their powerful neighbors. Even in their later history BCE, when many cosmopolitan influences had begun to affect them, they had produced no thinker of anything like the originality of Empedocles or Parmenides, of Plato or Aristotle.

At a much later stage in human history, Muhammad united many warring Arab tribes under the banner of Islam and within a few centuries the Muslim world was attracting Jewish and Christian scholars from Europe (e.g., Maimonides and the future Pope Sylvester II) before the founding of even the most ancient of the universities of Europe. Islam could hardly have attained even that temporary pre-eminence, however, but for its inheritance of Aristotle, whose work stimulated scholarly and scientifically-minded men in the Muslim world and provided them with the tools for philosophical, mathematical, and scientific enquiry according to the highest standards of their time.

The fact is that such intellectual, moral, and spiritual development is never attained overnight. It is in any case rare. Most people seldom think at all and even among the greatest of thinkers authentic thought is rarer than people generally tend to suppose. True, gigantic and sudden leaps seem sometimes to occur. In Christian Europe, for instance, in the thirteenth century, the Franciscans began as a band of simple mendicant friars whose rule did not permit them to own even a single book; by the end of the same century they were prominent in the intellectual leadership of the great centers of university learning at Paris, Oxford, and elsewhere. Such sudden leaps, however, occur after a long period of what we might call "silent" preparation. Like trees that suddenly shoot upward in spring, they have come prepared for the benefits of the sunshine and gentle showers that make possible their growth; they have not been idle during the long months of winter dormancy; they have been preparing themselves as with a good night's sleep we prepare ourselves for the adventures of the ensuing day.

The fine musical and other artistic perceptions of those who have been trained to develop such capacities open to them a vast range of experiences not available to their less fortunate brothers and sisters. The cultural expression of these perceptions varies of course from time to time and from place to place. It is of little more consequence in the long run than are styles of architecture or even of clothing, which vary according to circumstances, so that while Gothic churches and castles fit the face of northern Europe and the more northerly regions of the United States, they do not blend so well with the landscape of Southern California or of Greece, where Palladian or other such styles blend better with the landscape and the sunnier skies. So it is also in the realm of ethics. The moral sensibilities of those who have attained a higher awareness of ethical issues likewise open to them a wide range of experience not accessible to those in whom such sensibilities have not been developed. The differences are immense: at least as great as the differences between even the most primitive forms of human speech and the forms of communication available to even the higher simians.

So vast is the range of human capacity and attainment that man is better described as a process than as a species. Being human represents an enormous evolutionary development that has taken, as we have seen, something like three million years to traverse the distance between Lucy and the Dantes and Einsteins of our present millennium. We are a slice of evolutionary development rather than a species. What we have in common with all forms of life (a great ancient Indian insight that Schweitzer has expressed in his "reverence for life" maxim) is indeed wonderful; but the differences among human beings are more remarkable still.

Nor does the power attained by the most advanced of human beings consist merely in the invention of delectable fancies for the titillation of the mind, wafting it as on a magic carpet to the pleasures of the imagination. Authentic originality and creativity extend the *range* of human knowledge. The human brain, that three-pound mass we carry atop our bodies, contains large areas that seem to be "virgin soil" ready for development beyond our wildest dreams: a development that cannot be achieved by the old positivistic methodologies that once served well enough. By such positivistic methods, as Max Planck noted almost a century ago, physicists could not have discovered the quanta that are so central to modern physics and that have so immensely advanced and changed our understanding of the nature of the universe. That power of the human mind to transcend its present attainment and jump, so to speak, beyond itself is by far the most awesome of all its known capabilities. Yet it had its beginnings when our distant ancestors formed their first images, crude though they were, of a dimension of being beyond the one in which our human condition compels us to live out so much of our lives. That dimension, traditionally conceived as a realm of spirits, gods, and other agencies, is invisible to our eyes and intangible to our fingers, yet it affects our spiritual evolution at every point, however we choose to conceptualize it.

The model for an understanding of this other dimension of existence varies from culture to culture and from age to age. In our occidental heritage the concept of God as supreme, the creative source of all else, has dominated our three great religions: Judaism,

Christianity, and Islam. In the Orient the models that have generally prevailed are more pantheistic, to use a comparatively modern and certainly very Western term. Yet what is universal is the apprehension of another dimension that in one way or another impinges upon or intersects the empirical one with which we are habitually concerned.

Our relation to this other dimension of existence is full of paradox. To paraphrase one of the loveliest of Francis Thompson's poems *(The Kingdom of God),* it is a world which, though invisible, we see and, though intangible, we touch. Although, in Paul's idiom, we see it "through a glass darkly," it bears the promise of our seeing it "face to face" (I Corinthians 13:12). Like the men in Plato's allegory of the cave, we break loose from the chains that have kept our eyes fixed on a world that is the mere shadow of the world we now see and at first the splendor of that new world is so bright that it dazzles us till we become accustomed to its glory. As we mature spiritually we find ourselves on the edges of this other dimension until at last it breaks through upon us and becomes a part of our daily lives, bringing with it more poignant sorrows but more overwhelming joys than we could ever have known before. These sorrows and joys are symbolized respectively in orthodox Christian tradition by the Cross and the Resurrection of Christ.

In the same poem, Francis Thompson tells us that

> The angels keep their ancient places; —
> Turn but a stone, and start a wing!
> 'Tis ye, 'tis your estrangèd faces,
> That miss the many-splendoured thing.

We are not attuned to their voices; a mental cataract clouds our vision. Otherwise we could not miss what is going on in that other dimension, for

> The drift of pinions, would we hearken,
> Beats at our own clay-shuttered doors.

Who are these angels? Has the artistic fancy that has clothed them in shining wings ended by obscuring for us their reality? If so, what reality, if any, do they symbolize?

In the three major monotheistic religions the role of angels is traditionally important. Their importance is easily explained. For these religions, in their various ways, stress the notion of God as wholly other than, not to say aloof from, his creation. Angels play a necessary role as divine agents, messengers, or emissaries, to make the divine will known to humanity. In Islam this is especially notable, since historically, in reaction against the prevailing polytheism of the warring tribes Muhammed welded together, Islam arose with such a self-consciously acute preoccupation with the Oneness of God that this emphasis has remained embedded in the Muslim outlook in a special way. Allah communicates his will through angels who also watch over the affairs of men. The Old Testament (not least the Wisdom literature) however, is full of allusions to angels and in Hebrew tradition some of them are designated by name. Although in Christianity God is fully revealed to humankind in the person of Jesus Christ, the impending birth of Christ was announced to Mary by the angel Gabriel. How, indeed, other than by an angel could God, within the Hebrew tradition, have made known so special an intention as the birth of the Christ? Well may we focus, then, on angels as providing a model of the nature of the spiritual dimension that is the subject of our present enquiry.

Although in Christian tradition, with its markedly Hebrew heritage, the angelic hosts are of a different order of creation from humankind, and historically we must examine them as such (as we have done in Part I), we shall also have to take into account the possibility that they could represent a further stage in the long evolutionary process of human development with which this chapter began, taking Lucy as a milestone along the road. If we are to take seriously the reality of the evolutionary process that is attested to by so many fields of modern scientific enquiry, the likelihood that beings exist who are intellectually and spiritually more advanced than we are is surely overwhelming. The traditions about angels in all the major monotheistic religions have provided, to say the least, a good starting point for our enquiry. Like all the other great myths in religious literature they contain at least a pointer to an important truth. Our task now is to try to discover a way in which that truth can be made intelligible to us today. The hypothesis that angels could represent a kind of entity more advanced than humans is, to say the least, plausible enough to merit exploration. It is linked to the concept of the *Übermensch* or superman, which, as we are about to see, is not so exclusively "pagan" as is commonly supposed. At least some intimations of it are to be found in early Christian literature, a millennium and a half or more before Nietzsche and Darwin.

15

THE SUPERMAN IN ANCIENT AND MODERN THOUGHT

Why do you call a man who has been saved a superman?

TERTULLIAN (SECOND CENTURY, CE), AS REPORTED BY EPIPHANIUS

Let us now see whether, and if so in what way, angels might fit into modern ways of thought. Although the patristic and medieval understanding of angels as a separate creation, superior to man, fit the modes of thought of their day, they do not fit ours; nor can they be adapted in their entirety to any scheme of thought that takes seriously, as today we must, the evolutionary principle that we find everywhere in the universe. The angelology of Thomas Aquinas, for instance, although a brilliant intellectual construct in the thirteenth century, is inadequate, to say the least, for our time. It did provide the image of a race of superior beings not only endowed with capacities far beyond ours but, as "separate intelligences," having an individuality beyond that which man could expect to attain. Yet it was built upon an Aristotelian framework in which each created species is distinct from every other, so that there is no movement from one species toward a higher one representing an advance in an evolutionary process. Such an advance would have been as alien to the medieval mind as it would have been to Aristotle.

If angels are to be taken seriously today, they must represent a stage toward which at least some human beings might be moving, however slowly, in the course of a spiritual evolution. Of course

140

this is not to suggest anything so absurd as the idea that we are on the verge of being transformed into an angelic state. Even for the best of us that is likely to take a very long time in an evolutionary process that has taken millions of years to bring us from Lucy and our other primitive hominid ancestors to what we are today. But might not the concept of the superman, for example, be interpreted in such a way as to make the notion of angels more intelligible in a universe that is so manifestly ordered by an evolutionary principle? Let us see whether that be so.

Before embarking on a concept such as that of the superman, which must seem to many people today no less fanciful than that of an angel (since the superman is, after all, popularly conceived as a sort of "macho" angel), we ought to take seriously the charge that the notion of the superman is repugnant to the egalitarianism that many take to be a fundamental principle in a politically free society. Any suggestion of elitism naturally arouses suspicion in the minds of many, because the term has acquired a pejorative connotation. If, however, we look at the concept in perspective in terms of its origins and history, any elitism that we many find in it will be seen to be very benign.

What we all dislike in elitism in its pejorative sense is the arbitrary ranking of classes according to a hierarchy built upon highly prejudiced presuppositions. Categories of race, wealth, occupation, and sex are among the most pernicious of such arbitrary classifications. No sane person, however, doubts that some people are in fact more advanced in some ways than are others. Otherwise kindergarten and graduate school classes could be usefully united. All religions make similar distinctions between neophytes and those who are more mature in their spiritual pilgrimage. One does not on that account disparage immaturity any more than one disparages a sapling in comparing it to a giant oak, or a rosebud in setting it beside the full-blossomed rose that it will be tomorrow.

The Judaeo-Christian tradition and indeed the Bible itself is, as we have seen in the course of the present study, a panorama of elitism. The concept of election runs all through the Bible, Old Testament and New. The struggle goes back to Abel and Cain. Abraham pleads for Sodom on the grounds that he might be able to find some righteous people even there.[1] Israel is continually being purged. It is itself the chosen people of God, the elect nation, yet only a remnant within it succeed in surviving. The Christian Church claims to be the New Israel. Again the election motif is notably emphatic. True, it is not an elite of intellect alone; it is a moral elite. The 144,000 (a symbolic number of course) of the redeemed in the Book of Revelation clearly signifies a very select club indeed. The process of salvation is a highly selective process. Salvation is represented as very precious; hence the emphasis upon it. Were it less precious its attainment would not be so important. No religion in the world has ever seriously taught that human beings are *in fact* equal.

Elitism is so inseparable from religion that it is only a question of which kind of elitism is to be preferred. Elitism arising from heredity is ancient and an integral part not only of institutional religion in India, with its caste system, but of most societies. Such elitism is generally based on the simplistic view that qualities are genetically transmitted from parents to offspring in some more or less predictable way. While it is true that some traits of intellect or character may be genetically transmitted, the mode of their transmission is, to say the least, very much more complex than was formerly supposed. On the whole, therefore, the position of the religions which, like Christianity and Buddhism, ignore (at least in theory) any such hereditary basis for moral, intellectual, or spiritual quality is a salutary one. It does nothing, however, to diminish the inescapable fact that immense differences in spiritual maturity exist among individuals.

So with such important distinctions in mind between the arbitrary kinds of elitism that we all dislike, on the one hand, and, on the other, the difference in maturity that we all recognize as an inescapable reality, let us now look at the *kind* of elitism implicit in the concept of angels and supermen.

We can hardly doubt that the vogue of the term "superman" in modern literature and parlance is due to its use by that singularly original and much misunderstood German thinker, Friedrich Wilhelm Nietzsche (1844–1900), within whose philosophy it was a key term. Nietzsche came of a family in Saxony that had a long ecclesiastical tradition with clergymen on both the paternal and maternal sides. Not unexpectedly, he entered the University of Bonn as a theological student. He soon turned, however, to linguistic and philosophical studies, being much influenced by Schopenhauer (1788–1860). One of his works that was to be both a highly important milestone in his own thought and eventually an immense influence on European and American literature was produced between 1883 and 1885: *Also Sprach Zarathustra (Thus Spake*

Zarathustra), which bore the provocative subtitle, *Ein Buch für Alle und Keinen (A Book for All and None).* It was indeed a work that challenged the very foundations of traditional Judaeo-Christian values. With its revolt against these values and its exaltation of those of pagan antiquity, it shocked almost everybody. His was an elitist doctrine. Out of a gifted elite of men, strong in intellect and will, would arise, through what he called "the transvaluation of values," the *Übermensch,* a term englished as "superman."

The opposition that his thought evoked was inevitable. It came from many sides. At the end of the eighteenth century traditional religious values had seemed to many to be moribund if not dead, yet they were to stage an astonishing comeback. For the nineteenth century was to see, on the Protestant side, the rise of a missionary expansion throughout the world, while on the Catholic side the revival of interest in the Middle Ages through the influence of the Romantic movement was to predispose many to a reassessment of Catholic values. Not only were Newman and Pusey to lead the Tractarian movement in England; such was the revival of religious fervor in Roman Catholicism that it was to be possible in 1869–70, for the first time in three hundred years, to hold a General Council at Rome, now known as Vatican I, consisting of bishops from all over the world. In such a climate of widespread religious sentiment of one kind or another, Nietzsche's thought was bound both to offend many and to be widely misunderstood.

Opposition was inevitable from another quarter, however, for democratic ideas and socialistic movements were on the rise in Europe and the seemingly elitist aspect of Nietzsche's thought offended egalitarians of every kind. He was misunderstood as an arch-enemy of religion, but while destroying the foundation of one stage of the religious consciousness he was providing another as the basis for (some might contend) a far higher stage. That his philosophy is elitist is indisputable, as we have seen, but worthwhile religion has an elitist *aspect,* as has worthwhile education. Superficial readers, however, who often acquainted themselves with him only at second hand, thought of him as exalting might over right, brute strength over mental refinement and moral sensitivity. Some even imagined him to be a champion of Prussian imperialism, a particularly wrongheaded notion since Nietzsche had a somewhat poor opinion of his compatriots and was disposed, rather, to the vision of the "good European."

Although Nietzsche eventually came to be better understood, at least among scholars in Europe and America, his notion of the "superman" is still often taken to be more novel than in fact it is.

The term *hyperanthrōpos,* which means literally "hyper-man" or "super-man", is found in Lucian, a pagan satirist of the second century of the Christian Era. It is just possible, indeed, that Nietzsche drew the term *Übermensch* from him or some other pagan source. More unexpectedly, however, the term occurs also in early Christian literature. Although by the end of the first century expectations of a speedy end of the age had tended to decline, an apocalyptic movement in the second part of the second century, led by one Montanus, was directed against the increasingly institutionalist tendencies in the Church. The Montanists emphasized the Gospel promise that the Lord would send the Paraclete, the Holy Spirit, and they claimed that they were now living in the age of the Paraclete, which they understood as the last age before the end of time. Montanus believed himself to be the special instrument of the Holy Spirit. We learn from Epiphanius, a fourth-century Church Father, that among the prophetic proclamations of Montanus that he knew was one in which the Holy Spirit spoke as follows: "Why do you call a man who has been saved a superman? (*ti legeis ton hyper anthrōpon sōzomenon?*) The Paraclete says that the righteous [i.e., the Spirit-filled] shall shine a hundred times more strongly than the sun and the little ones among you that have been saved [i.e., the mere adherents of the movement] shall shine a hundred times more than the moon."[2]

Montanism went beyond any mere general expectation of a restoration of humanity. Humanity was not to be restored; it was to be advanced to a higher level: the level of the *hyperanthrōpos,* the superman. According to John (John 14:12), Jesus had suggested that his disciples, after the Holy Spirit had come, would do even more marvelous works than he did himself. Those who were Spirit-filled were to belong to a new race, a race evolved *out of* humanity yet transcending humanity as we know it. Here, then, is an early Christian formulation of the notion of the superman: a new race made possible through Christ and the presence of the Holy Spirit whom he had sent to the Church.

Predictably, as the Church's institutionalism hardened, notions of a new race and a new age receded; nevertheless, we find echoes of the Montanist outlook in some of the mystics. The twelfth-century Joachim of Fiore, for instance, made a pilgrimage as a young man to the Holy Land, where he experienced a conversion that led to his entering the Cistercian Order. He later founded a monastery of his own that received papal approval in 1196. His sanctity was widely recognized. Dante alluded to him as *di spirito profetico dotato*. Like Francis of Assisi of the following century he was critical of the ecclesiastical establishment and some of his teachings were duly condemned by the Lateran Council in 1215.

Prominent in Joachim's teaching was the doctrine that the Holy Spirit would usher in a new age in which the faithful would be gradually enlightened by the workings of an inner light. First they had had to live under the Law; then through Christ they had been introduced to the freedom of the Gospel and the workings of grace; but they were to progress still further through the direct working of the Holy Spirit, which would gradually transform humanity. According to Joachim, as to Montanus, the human race is not being restored; it is making specific progress to a more advanced stage of evolution.

The nature of that more advanced stage of evolution is expressed in the language Joachim adopts: those who attain it are called *angelici spiritus,* angelic spirits; they are beyond humanity as we know it. The influence of Joachim's teaching persisted in many byways inside and outside the medieval Catholic Church. To the mainstream of Christian thought and practice it must have seemed no doubt visionary and wild. Spiritual evolution as he envisioned it was not an accustomed way of thinking in his time or for long afterwards.

Joachim's age was less optimistic than the nineteenth century, which became so intoxicated with evolutionism that some saw everything in one way or another as steadily moving in a spiral of progress. Twentieth-century thinkers have been generally much more chary of the idea of progress. This has been partly because of devastating wars and other catastrophes but also because the rise of democratic ideas has conditioned many people to look for a wider distribution of the enjoyment of goods proper to our present state rather than to the leap of a few to a higher order.

As Marshall McLuhan has called to our attention, modern technology, despite the many good things it has brought to us, paradoxically promotes the tendency to push us back into tribalism rather than forward into individualism. When people read less and less and watch television more and more, an entire nation of a quarter of a billion inhabitants is bound together by what happens at the Rose Bowl and their mind-set is formed by what a national network pumps into them. Of course many men and women even in such a dreary scenario transcend it as vivacious minds always will; nevertheless, such conditions can hardly be called conducive to *widespread* preoccupation with advancing to a higher stage of evolution such as is implied in the concept of the superman either in its ancient or in its nineteenth-century form. The medieval period was for other reasons (although in fact it was in its own way far more technologically advanced than some suppose) also ill-prepared for evolutionary concepts. In any case, however, evolutionary leaps of any kind are not only more gradual than one might expect; they entail huge losses alongside seemingly meager gains.

Interest in evolution, both in history and in biology, antedated Darwin by several generations. Kant, in a paper published in 1755, speculated that the immortal soul might travel, in the course of an infinity of time, from one planet to another. He suggested that some planets might be in an embryonic state, being readied to accommodate us when we have completed our sojourn on earth. Of course this was, as well he recognized, mere fanciful speculation; but it shows a trend in the thinking of great minds long before the overwhelming evidence for an evolutionary principle in the universe was to be provided. An eccentric Scottish judge, Lord Monboddo, writing almost a century before Darwin's book *On the Origin of Species* was published in 1859, proposed that at one time man had had a tail like other mammals. Long before the discovery of fossil evidence, he had a "hunch" about our relation to the simians.

Adumbrations of such insights are to be found also in Germany, for example in the writings of one Berthold Heinrich Brockes early in the eighteenth century, who toys with the notion that the monkey could be considered a distant relative of man. "What," he asks, "must be the length of the spiritual ladder that has so many rungs up and down?" Franz von Baader, as early as 1834, was writing about evolution as a principle in human history, applying it even to the history of man's salvation.

No doubt many such forerunners of modern evolutionary thinking were too optimistic, sometimes taking the next stage to be almost round the corner and ready to come into full view. They saw, however, glimmerings of the idea of the superman, which, we have seen, had simmered for long in the background of ancient and medieval thought and that Nietzsche eventually was to develop and make so influential in literary and other circles.

Angels are even more ancient in human thought. As ambassadors of God and attendants round the divine throne they would seem to qualify *par excellence* as supermen. Are we to take them as functioning in that way? When Pascal calls man a chimera, half-angel, half-beast, is he seeing in his own way the panorama of spiritual evolution? Is he seeing that we are half way toward the angelic status while being still only half way out of the bestial one? Might not bodhisattvas (conceived as human beings qualified for buddhahood but generously choosing to dally with us to help in our spiritual advancement) likewise so function? Might the androgynous ideal we glanced at in an earlier chapter be realizable at a later stage of our evolution, so ultimately resolving to perfection the profound and multifaceted problems of our human sexuality? We shall consider this aspect of our study in greater detail in a later chapter.

But let us look at what actually happened when Darwin's epoch-making *On the Origin of Species by Means of Natural Selection, or the Preservation of Favoured Races in the Struggle for Life* appeared on November 24, 1859. The entire edition of 1,250 copies (much larger in proportion to the smaller reading public than it would signify today) was exhausted on the day of issue. The storm it created is well known, as is the famous duel on June 30 of the following year between T. H. Huxley and Bishop Wilberforce at a meeting of the British Association in Oxford. That attack on biological evolution occurred some sixty-five years before the even more notorious Scopes trial in Tennessee. Less well known is the rapidity of the acclaim of Darwin's book in Marxist circles as a new instrument in the demolition of Christian anthropology. On December 12, 1859, less than three weeks after the publication of the book, Engels wrote a letter to Marx announcing its importance and interpreting it as showing human history as a continuation of natural history and therefore providing for the demolition of all idealistic Hegelian notions and all pious Christian beliefs about supranatural purposes at work behind the scenes. All could be reducible to what the Victorians generally classified as "materialism."

It happened that Marx was preoccupied with various problems at the time, but about a year later he did report in a letter to Engels that he had at last found time to read Darwin and declared that the English naturalist had indeed established the basis in natural history for their theory of dialectical materialism. Soon Darwinism came to be widely understood in Europe as an ally of the new Marxist materialistic socialism. The Marxists, however, had interpreted Darwin in a special way, fitting him into their own ideology rather than examining his thought in any scientifically careful way. Not seeing, or not wishing to see, that Darwinian theory is susceptible to more than one interpretation regarding the future of humankind, they cavalierly appropriated it under their own banner.

Engels, Moses Hess, and other Marxist pioneers, following the materialistic humanism propounded by Feuerbach, disliked and openly attacked the entire notion of the *Übermensch* when it came into vogue. For they saw it as implying evolution to a stage *beyond* man and therefore nonhuman, while they professed to be helping, rather, to bring man as he is into focus. The notion of suprahumanity carried with it a flavor of ideas such as "God" and "afterlife" that they wished specifically to reject. It had overtones of the "supernatural" that they wanted to remove from the vocabulary altogether or invest with a negative, not to say comical, character. Of course in time there were some modifications of the cruder forms of Marxism in its early stages, but it never lost its simplistic reliance on a thoroughly doctrinaire anthropology and its facile assumption that Darwinism can be interpreted only in a grossly "materialistic" way. They could not entertain, for example, the possibility that the suprahuman condition envisioned by Nietzsche and others could serve as the means of preserving elements of humanity as we know it, somewhat as our present state (half-angel, half-beast) has preserved our biological affinity with other mammals despite our transcending them in so many obvious ways.

True, Nietzsche himself disowned many of the interpretations of his superman. Yet he was not consistent in his repudiation, for example, of the superman as a sort of strong-willed saintly genius, for at times this is precisely how he presented him. In *The Birth of Tragedy,* for instance, after denying that the state and humanity itself exist only for their own sake, he goes on to affirm that the goal lies in the lonely ones, "the saints and artists" and that this goal clearly points beyond humanity. Their uniqueness does not exist *for* humanity; humanity exists, rather, as a fulcrum providing leverage for their oars as they row toward their destination, which entails the surpassing of humanity.

But what is humanity? What is this "man" that is on his way to a higher stage? He is already in process. The question is whether the process will achieve Nietzsche's vision of it or not, for there can be no guarantee. Nietzsche is, rather, issuing a clarion call to humanity to see that its destiny lies beyond its present state. If the achievement had been inevitable, then the dinosaur and other extinct species would have had a less tragic ending. Of course Nietzsche was like others in misunderstanding and therefore misinterpreting Darwin at some points. Nevertheless, he attacked what he took to be the one-sidedness of Darwin's theory on the ground that Darwin had failed to perceive the role that freedom plays in human action. Freedom is not unique to humanity, but human freedom is qualitatively greater than that to be found in the lower forms of life with which Darwin, as befitted his professional preoccupation, was primarily concerned. Nietzsche, although plainly much indebted to Darwin, was highly critical of him.

Nietzsche's vision of the superman, great contribution though it is to human thought, is so open-ended as to lack the precision needed to make its meaning clear. He is never entirely clear about what sort of virtues are to be transvalued and so transmogrified. Sometimes the American transcendentalists seem to qualify as models, with Emerson in the forefront; sometimes Napoleon seems to embody better the ideal of the *Übermensch*. To this Nietzsche could reply, indeed, that in the nature of the case one can no more predict what the superman is to be than could the most advanced among our hominid ancestors have specified the direction toward which they were aiming or the nature of the qualities that were to be acclaimed as cultivated and civilized. Yet we do need some sort of principle to define the achievement of what we are being encouraged to pursue. Certainly it is not brute strength or anything of the sort. Yet it is no less certainly not the Christian virtues of humility and self-abnegation *as traditionally understood*. Might it then be defined as the achievement of superior mental organization such as would lead to liberation from the constraints of enslaving forms of morality and constricting alleys of thought? Yes indeed, that much is plain. But precisely wherein lie the enslavements to be overcome? We need a model of some kind or at least the means to construct an ideal. Jesus, as traditionally depicted, certainly will not do for Nietzsche, but then to what extent precisely, in face of the results of New Testament scholarship, must we be bound by the traditional understanding of the historic Jesus?

Nietzsche denigrated traditional Christian ethics on at least two counts. In the first place he saw it as stultified and decrepit. All great ethical and religious systems as they persist through the centuries tend to petrify, losing the life-spring that once gave them their vitality and invested them with their original significance. Nietzsche's other critique of Christian ethics is, however, more basic. He perceived the Christian injunctions and counsels set forth in the Gospels and attributed to Jesus as a "slave morality." The Sermon on the Mount, for instance, which is a collection of the moral aphorisms and other sayings that are reported as typical of the Master's teachings, counsels the disciples "to turn the other cheek." Instead of calling for courage and boldness they exalt meekness, for "the meek shall inherit the earth." Mercy is commended because by showing mercy one is likely to have mercy shown to oneself. The "poor in spirit" (*hoi ptōchoi tō pneumati*) are said to be happy because the kingdom of heaven is theirs. Is not all this calculated to turn morally healthy and vigorous people into weaklings? Instead of ennobling men and women, does not it end, rather, by enslaving them?

To understand the question raised here we must see the ethical teaching attributed to Jesus in the Gospels in its historical context and background. Jesus was deeply rooted in the life of his people and in the outlook bequeathed to them by their circumstances and their Hebrew heritage. The Hebrews had been from very early times accustomed to the cruel yoke of slavery. When they did escape from the Egyptians they were still poor and vulnerable, surrounded by powerful neighbors to whose military might they were exposed on all sides. Their primary concern, not unnaturally, was survival. Even their more prosperous periods of peace and comparative independence afforded them scant opportunity for the cultivation of that sort of society in which they might have developed the kind of virtues that Nietzsche could have admired. Palestine in the time of Jesus was once again under foreign occupation, now as an outpost of the great Roman Empire. When Jesus was giving moral counsel to his disciples he was doing so in terms of their own situation. He was telling them in powerful language what, in a way, they already knew in their hearts. Indeed, not only is the ethical teaching of Jesus as recorded in the Gospels geared to his own people's circumstance and heritage; it is already implicit and often explicit in the Hebrew heritage itself. His admonitions are not infrequently actual quotations from the Hebrew scriptures. Whatever is original in the Gospels, it is not to be sought in the ethical teaching. This is the heritage with which the Christian Way started out as it spread from Jerusalem to the Gentile world.

Although no doubt the ethical teaching of the Gospels much influenced early converts to the Christian Way (for are not we all in one way or another slaves to our circumstances?), it was not any new or daring element in the ethical teaching that attracted converts. It was the *kerygma:* the proclamation that Christ had risen and through him one could hope to rise to new life. The Christian Way was about the light and love that living with Christ in one's heart could bring about. Through the action of the Holy Spirit in the life of the Christian community, converts felt the beat of a new tune: the heartbeat of new hope.

The moral implications of such a revolutionary idea were not necessarily spelled out, but whatever they were they must have gone far beyond the characteristic sayings of Jesus as recorded, for example, in the Sermon on the Mount. By following these teachings, which are generally prudential, one *survives:* no small achievement when the world is set against you. But the promise of Jesus that he would rise from the dead, which the first apostles believed to have been fulfilled and took as the center and ground of their apostolic proclamation, is not a mere promise of survival; it is the promise of *arrival* at a new kind of life: "we shall be changed . . . because our present perishable nature must put on imperishability and this mortal nature must put on immortality" (I Corinthians 15:52f.) Turning the other cheek is by no means bad or unneeded moral advice; but it is not enough to serve as a moral lodestar for the Christian enterprise of achieving such new life in Christ. That takes a moral quantum leap. Morals for survival are patently inadequate for becoming a *hyperanthrōpos* and attaining immortality with Christ.

Nietzsche, although he must have known something about the great developments in the nineteenth century, not least in his own Germany, seems to have lacked the perspective needed to appreciate the point I have just made. He died in 1900, six years before the appearance, for example, of Albert Schweitzer's epoch-making study of the historical Jesus, which was published in 1906 under the title *Von Reimarus zu Wrede,* translated in the English edition of 1910 as *The Quest of the Historical Jesus.* This and later critical New Testament studies made it more difficult to accept the comparatively simplistic understanding of Christian ethics that even so great a mind as Nietzsche's could regard as all that Christianity could offer.

The precepts of the Sermon on the Mount, for instance, are

plainly, as Nietzsche perceived, for the "herd"; and that the herd as such needs guidance must surely go without saying. But no less surely do those who are called to new life in Christ and destined for immortality need other guidance. They need to learn a new kind of courage, a new sort of resourcefulness, and to acquire a new *genre* of moral qualities along with the old, traditional ethic of the Sermon on the Mount. The latter is by no means irrelevant; for the adventure of arrival at the new life in Christ one must also survive. What one must learn about office routine is not at all irrelevant to what an industrial entrepreneur must learn; but it is certainly not enough for him. So the "herd" ethic that Nietzsche found so inadequate in the Christian ethic as he understood it is indeed a dimension of the Christian life but by no means exhausts its riches. It demands other dimensions.

If, then, we think in evolutionary terms, why should not the notion of the superman, which so captured the imagination of Ibsen and Shaw and so many other Victorian and Edwardian writers, be christened? We have seen that it has antecedents in early Christian thought and speech. Might not, then, the long tradition of angels that is writ so deep in the Bible and has so much influenced all the three great monotheistic religions be made more intelligible by being understood as referring to a more *advanced* state of being than our own: a state already achieved in a realm presently beyond us but which we may hope to reach through Christ?

The superiority of beings more advanced than we, call them what we will, must be in the last resort a superiority in the quality of their love. The angels, according to Thomas, are higher than we in intelligence. Unhampered by corporeality, they can apprehend more clearly and distinctly than we can and grasp reality more effectively. (Here as so often in Thomas we see how sympathetic he is to some aspects of Neo-Platonism.) Yet their superiority lies not only in their greater cognitive capacity but also and much more in their greater capacity for love: the love that surpasses intellectual knowledge. This love that surpasses knowledge is itself, however, a *kind* of knowledge, for it confers knowledge of a sort that is inaccessible to intellect alone.

23. ANGELS WEEPING AT THE DEATH OF CHRIST.
Giotto di Bondone (1266–1337), *Deposition of Christ from the Cross.*
Cappella dell'Arena, Padua.

24. ABRAHAM! YOU ARE NOT TO DO IT!
Filippo Brunelleschi (1377–1446), *Sacrifice of Isaac*. Bargello, Florence.

25. MARY BORNE BY ANGELS.
Tiziano Vecellio (1489–1576),
Ascension of the Virgin.
Frari, Venice.

26. ISLAMIC ANGEL GREETING MARY.
Annunciation. Edinburgh University.

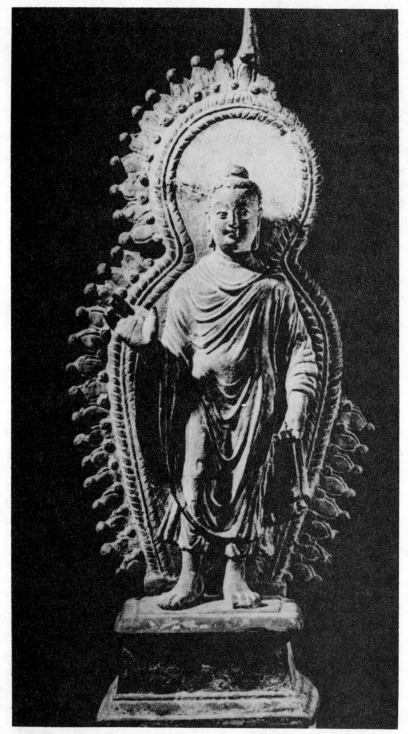

27. BODHISATTVA.
Bronze. Victoria and Albert Museum, London.

28. SOME HINDU DEVAS.

157

29. REBELS IN HEAVEN.
Domenico Beccafumi (1485–1551), *Fall of Angels*.
Pinacoteca Nationale, Siena.

30. A DEVIL AMONG THE ANGELS.
Matthias Grunewald (15th century), *Altar of Isenheim.* Colmar, France.

31. WINGED DEVILS.
William Blake (1757–1827). Tate Gallery, London.

32. THE DEVIL WITH A HALO.
Temptation of Job. Bibliothèque
royale, Paris.

16

PARANORMAL EXPERIENCES SUCH AS COMMUNICATION WITH THE DEPARTED

> In the collection of facts, one cannot be overcautious. But in the invention of theories, especially in a field so peculiar as ours, where analogies drawn from the existing sciences are almost useless, a canny and sober circumspection would be the greatest mistake.
>
> H. H. PRICE, IN HIS PRESIDENTIAL ADDRESS TO THE SOCIETY FOR PSYCHICAL RESEARCH, 1939

Whatever angels may or may not be, they certainly belong to the range of what is commonly called "paranormal" experience. That is to say, not only do they appear at best no more than occasionally and in the experience of a limited number of people; they do not conform to the empirical world as we commonly apprehend it in waking life. The realm of experience that we call "normal" is that with which we are (at least primarily) concerned when we cook a breakfast of bacon and eggs or go out to start the car in the driveway.

This obvious fact raises at once, however, a question: What determines "the normal" and distinguishes it from "the paranormal"? A detailed discussion of this very difficult philosophical question is beyond the scope of this book and unnecessary. We should note, nevertheless, certain essential points. If a highly intelligent medieval monk were to be able to see a moden photostatic machine turning out a thousand copies of a page of manuscript in a few minutes he might well account the experience a paranor-

161

mal one. He could be shown, however, that the same principles he and others of his day were using in making and using agricultural implements were being employed in the photostatic copier, and once he had been shown this he could no longer account the latter as falling beyond the scope of "normal" experience. The same principles for verification and falsification could have been used in both cases. The same principles could not have been used, however, to investigate, say, the submicroscopic world; nor could the methodologies used in *any* physics, Newtonian or otherwise, work in biology, nor again would the latter work in psychology.

For more than a century, the British and American societies for psychical research have been examining paranormal phenomena with the same meticulous care that scientists would give to inquiries in any field. This kind of laborious investigation, case by case, has led to very interesting results. Hypnosis, for example, is now a very widely recognized phenomenon, the importance and practical use of which no educated person today can doubt. Telepathy has been shown to be a fairly common occurrence. That a mother should wake up in the middle of the night in San Francisco in great distress at a dream she has had of her son's being killed in London and that this should turn out to have happened at precisely the hour of her waking in her distress hardly raises an eyebrow among those who have seriously studied such "paranormal" phenomena. Hypnosis is all but commonplace, being used for anaesthesia in childbirth and elsewhere in the practice of medicine and surgery. Probably most people, in urban areas at least, have seen a show at one time or another in which a hypnotist has taken volunteers to the stage and caused them, under hypnosis, to do exactly as he commands. We need hardly be reminded that heterosuggestion, a less dramatic form of hypnosis, is in extensive daily use in the advertising media.

The occurrence of such phenomena, which were widely suspect not so very long ago, is now beyond cavil. What may be disputable is the nature of the process by which they work. Such inquiries into paranormal experience are certainly relevant to our central purpose. If, in our study of angelology, we were to overlook the area of paranormal experience, we should be almost like students of music who overlooked the physical and psychological conditions that make musical appreciation possible and without which a person might discern no difference between music played by the New York Philharmonic and that rendered on a barrel organ.

Is there then a mental "faculty" or sensitivity for apprehending paranormal phenomena such as "an ear for music"? To say the very least, that would appear to be the case. But if so, how does it work? By what process is telepathy, for example, accomplished? Some researchers in the field have proposed that this type of communication takes place at a purely mental level, apart from the brain. More persuasive to some is the view long ago proposed by Thouless and Wiesner (two pioneers in the field and very competent investigators) that under certain conditions I, who regularly control my own brain, may achieve some degree of control of another's brain and exercise that control. While, however, telepathy sometimes occurs in ways that suggest such intentional control, at other times (perhaps oftener) it seems to occur on an unconscious level. Many of us have had the embarrassing experience, for instance, of meeting a person for the first time and, wishing to make conversation, choosing the most unfortunate of subjects: the one much on the other person's mind and emotionally troubling him or her. For instance, one might talk of drug addiction, since it had been prominently mentioned on the six o'clock news, only to discover that the other person's son or daughter had been arrested the previous day on a drug-trafficking charge. Or one might even talk of a murder story one had just read and find later that the person to whom we had been introduced was the wife of a man under arrest on suspicion of murder. Why does one come to choose, out of all possible topics, such a singularly unfortunate one? No civilized human being would intentionally or knowingly do anything of the sort. It would seem that the mental preoccupation of the distressed person had been somehow transferred to the person unwittingly perpetrating the outrage. We all know, too, that between persons meeting for the first time and sexually attracted to one another a great deal of communication may occur without any linguistic expression at all, not even "body language." How does such thought-transference take place?

Thouless and Wiesner used the Greek letter *psi* (ψ) to denote all paranormal faculties. They suggested, further, that such faculties have more than one aspect; for example, a cognitive aspect, which they designated *psi-gamma* ($\psi\gamma$) and a motor aspect, *psi-kappa* ($\psi\kappa$). While we need not be committed to their particular explanation of the processes involved in extra-sensory perception (ESP) (although I think it persuasive) we cannot ignore ESP phenomena that have become so well attested and so thoroughly studied in such a scientific way by the societies for psychical research. How we choose to interpret them is another matter.

Since from time immemorial men and women have had experiences of the presence (in dreams or otherwise) of their departed ancestors or friends, the claim that contact had been made with such persons in a "spirit world" was of course one that had to be scientifically explored along with other paranormal experiences. Such exploration yielded some very remarkable results. It led to widespread, renewed interest in what came to be called spiritualism or spiritism, the popularity of which came in waves, reaching a climax during and after World War I, when so many families were suddenly bereaved. Alas, spiritualistic séances turned out to be financially a very profitable enterprise for charlatans and hoaxters, inevitably heaping notoriety and ridicule on the whole concept of communication with "the other side." Moreover, since the spiritualist movement often took on a specifically religious guise, sometimes with an almost conventional church setting and the paraphernalia of worship, the clergy of the mainstream churches, who obviously had a vested interest in denigrating it, often joined in the efforts to discredit the movement in principle instead of criticizing its widespread abuse.

The relevance of the whole area to our central theme is, we have already maintained, plain enough. Belief in a realm of such spirits (ancestors or friends) is very ancient and is a well-known aspect of the shamanism that has been practiced for thousands of years in primitive societies all over the world and is still widely practiced. Belief in angels might well spring from the same source. Such beings, if they exist at all, might well be the manifestations of such a spirit-realm. So all psi phenomena, including such "spiritualistic" ones, come within the scope of our subject. The angelic presences that some people claim to have so distinctly felt might well belong to the same realm as do the phenomena that spiritualists claim, sometimes almost casually, to encounter, and that they hold to be in fact relatives and friends. If angels do have any ontologically independent existence apart from our own minds, may not they be our kindly disposed ancestors or friends? If there is any truth in spiritualistic claims, and if my aunt was angelically benevolent in life, why should she not be angelically benevolent still, and so appear to me as an angel?

The recognition of any dimension of existence other than the empirical one would make the ontological reality of angels instantly plausible. One would wish to hear more of the way in which one distinguished one entity from another, but that would be a comparatively minor question. So if the phenomenon of a "spirit world" of any kind were established, the entire field of angelology would take on a different aspect. It would be taken seriously even by those who had never had any experience they would describe in any such terms, much as a zoologist in the past who had never learned of the existence of kangaroos would take seriously the possibility presented to him by someone who claimed to have seen one and could describe it in some technical detail.

The term "telepathy" appears to have been coined by F.W.H Myers, pioneer in the field of psychical research, whose work *Human Personality and Its Survival of Bodily Death* is recognized to be a classic in the field. The phenomenon of thought-reading or thought-transference to which it refers is, however, one that has been recognized from the earliest periods of recorded human history, expressed in a popular belief that certain individuals have a special gift or faculty, denied to the majority of us, by means of which they can tell what another person is thinking. Along with this goes also an ancient belief in what was often called "second sight" and is now more generally called "clairvoyance": the ability to perceive what is beyond ordinary sense-perception, such as the state of another person's most hidden thoughts and emotions.

That the academic world of scholars and scientists should have been skeptical about such phenomena was of course predictable. It was also laudable, for scholars and scientists are critical *par métier* and ought to be. What Myers and the other founders of the British Society for Psychical Research evoked, however, was not mere skepticism but bitter hostility and sometimes even contempt. Not only were the founders possessed of well-trained minds; early members of and contributors to the society included some very distinguished names in scholarship and the sciences. Their eminence, however, seems only to have exacerbated the hostility. That untrained minds should dabble in such speculations perhaps seemed more forgivable than that eminent scholars and scientists should be examining paranormal phenomena with all the seriousness they would have devoted to academically reputable investigations. The misgivings of the conventional scholars and scientists is understandable, however, for charlatanry had brought great notoriety to "dabblers in the occult."

The founders included (besides Myers) Henry Sidgwick, a prominent Cambridge philosopher in his day, and Sir William Barrett, a Dublin professor of physics. Early members and contributors included, among physicists, Sir Oliver Lodge and Lord Rayleigh; among biologists, Hans Driesch; among psychologists, William James (who was also involved in the foundation of the American Society) and William McDougall; Henri Bergson, one of the most internationally renowned among French philosophers of his day, and Charles Richet, a French Nobel laureate in physiology. Somewhat later came philosophers such as C. D. Broad, H. H. Price, and C. J. Ducasse, biologists such as Sir Alister Hardy, and psychologists such as Gardner Murphy and R. H. Thouless.

Myers wrote that he "had at first a great repugnance to studying the phenomena alleged by the spiritualists."[1] Born in 1843, he was from an early age fascinated by classical languages and literature and in 1865 became a lecturer in classics at his Cambridge college (Trinity). Disillusioned with the Church as he had known it, he asked his favorite teacher, Henry Sidgwick, whether he thought that the study of observable psychic phenomena might help toward an understanding of the universe. Sidgwick gave him cautious encouragement and in spite of the distaste Myers felt for the type of person whom he found in the role of psychic "medium" he persisted, although for some time rather unenthusiastically, in his investigations. In the fall of 1873, however, he believed he had come across for the first time a "personal experience of forces unknown to science." Some years later he claimed to have received a communication from a very dear friend who had died in 1876. This experience convinced him conclusively that human beings survive bodily death. In 1882 the British Society for Psychical Research was founded to investigate all paranormal phenomena, including cases of alleged evidence for survival of bodily death. Myers died in Rome in 1901 (during his year as president of the society he had helped to found) and was buried in Keswick, Cumberland, his birthplace.

Myers was not technically trained in philosophy and his approach to the subject reflects this at certain points. For example, a central philosophical question in relation to alleged bodily survival after death would be: what precisely is it that survives bodily death? To say with Myers that it is personality raises an obvious problem, for personality (a comparatively modern concept, by the way) is not a constant but itself a phenomenon that can change considerably even within the space of a decade of any individual's life, and in some cases and to some extent even from day to day according to one's mood. My friends tell me that my personality changes markedly when I engage in animated conversation in French. It has certainly changed enormously since, say, the age of three. Whatever it is that might survive bodily death, therefore, cannot be my personality.

What if, say, my mother were to visit me from "the other side"? Critics would naturally ask: In which of her personalities that I had known throughout my life, from when she was a comparatively young woman till finally she was an octogenarian, was her presence manifested to me? Was it the vivacious one of her earlier years, or the more sedately quiet one of her old age? In any case, since her personality like everyone else's changed so much in the course of a few decades, is it not likely to have changed at least as much again by this time, some decades after her bodily death?

Plainly, if anything is to survive physical death, it must be a more constant entity lying behind all "psychic apparel." In traditional Christian terminology it is the "soul" *(nephesh, psychē)* that is this enduring entity. In the upanishadic thought of ancient India it is not so simple as that. Not only is the physical body discarded like a sheath; there are several "layers" of bodies to be discarded before coming to the essential "core": the inmost "self" which alone endures through a long chain of embodiments.

The importance of such questions lies in the fact that before one is to set about "proving" something about paranormal phenomena one should be able to specify precisely what one hopes to prove or disprove. To claim to prove that my mother came to me from "the other side" wearing the dress I last saw her wear some decades ago would be very different from claiming to establish that her presence was manifested in no such way, and that indeed she did not have the appearance of a flesh-and-blood embodiment at all.

This leads us to a further question that bears directly upon our main concern in this book. That I might recognize a dear friend even in the strangest circumstances is intelligible in principle. But how, when I claim to experience an angelic presence *for the first time,* can I identify the presence as that of an angel? What is it that I could possibly be *recognizing?* An image drawn from, say, my reading of Isaiah's vision or of an angel as described in the Apocalypse? Or the picture of an angel in Christian art?

But all these are patently verbal metaphors or iconographic

devices which try, however feebly, to express a paranormal phenomenon in terms of "normal" sensory perception. If asked how
many wings my angelic visitant had, could I give a certain number
in reply? Or the color of the angel or the texture or anything else
that I might be asked about a human or other animal embodiment?
If I did, my answer would certainly be suspect, for my source would
obviously be the poetry of the Bible or the visual imagination of a
painter or sculptor. I would say, of course, that I did not see or
hear the angel as one hears or sees a human being and that I
experienced, rather, a presence; but how could I identify it as the
presence of an angel, never before having encountered one? I
could not even identify my own father or mother in the flesh if I
had never before seen them. Furthermore, if, as the New Testament
writer reminds us, "no man hath seen God at any time" (I John
4:12), how precisely could one be said to *recognize* one of his
messengers, the angels?

To all this one might reply that the case would have some
similarity to that of encountering extraterrestrial intelligent life in
an embodiment very different from ours. The embodiment, whatever it might be, would in itself provide little clue to the nature of
the entity or of the character of the intelligence it embodied. What
causes a dog to submit to and obey the commands of his master,
acknowledging in his own fashion the master's superiority, surely
cannot have anything to do with the fact that his master, like all
humans, is a biped standing erect and carrying his brain aloft. That
would not in itself inspire the fidelity for which dogs are renowned.
No, the superiority the dog instinctively recognizes in his master
must come to be acknowledged, rather, by some form of communication that passes from master to dog. True, once this has been
accomplished the dog no doubt recognizes the presence of his
master by scent and otherwise, but my dog cannot have come to
acknowledge me as his master by reason of my smell or any other
such attribute. On the contrary, the acknowledgement on his part
must have been evoked in the first place by the love and concern
he has somehow detected as issuing from me and my competence
to care for him. If we were to encounter for the first time an
extraterrestrial entity of clearly superior intelligence and nobler
character than is generally found within the human race, the
acknowledgement of its superiority would surely spring from some
such communication, not from its embodiment, whatever that
might be. A claim to have encountered an angelic entity would have

to be grounded in the nature of the communication received. Even then, one would surely have to stipulate that one's specific identification of the entity as an angel would have sprung from what one has learned about angels from the Bible or tradition. Yet one could not preclude the possibility that the entity was, for example, a being more advanced in evolutionary development: perhaps as far in advance of *homo sapiens* as Lucy is behind us.

That the "unconscious" plays a crucial role in all psychic phenomena seems plain. But what precisely are we to understand by the term, which Freud has made so popular? The "unconscious" as the term has been traditionally used in philosophy is simply the opposite of "conscious." Freud not only was careful to establish his own specific usage of the term, but went on to make a further distinction between two separate senses of it; these he designates by the terms *Ucs.* and *Pcs.* respectively.[2] Both refer to the notion that everything psychic exists as unconscious. The former, however, is "incapable of consciousness," while the latter's excitations, after the observance of certain rules, are capable of reaching the conscious level. Freud likens the Pcs. system to a screen between the Ucs. system and consciousness. Elsewhere he also distinguishes from one another the "descriptive, dynamic, and systematic meanings" of the terms. Jung uses the term "unconscious" differently. For him it is that part of the psyche that is to be regarded as undeveloped rather than as repressed. It includes both the personal factor and the collective factor: the dispositions inherited genetically from ancestors.

Both men's viewpoints—but especially Jung's—suggest that we could be open to all sorts of psychic influences, good and bad, floating around, so to speak, in a common psychic pool. For at this unconscious level of mental life the boundaries of "your" psyche and "mine" seem to be much less clearly marked, to say the least, than they are at the conscious level. That would go some way toward explaining why telepathic communication is much less likely to occur concerning intellectual matters than concerning emotional ones. Lovers understand one another with a minimum of speech and often with none at all. For them "the waters woo" and "the night replies."[3] At an intellectual level much more discursive communication is needed. So while one often hears of telepathic communication where intense emotions are involved, one rarely if ever hears of, say, an Oxford mathematician's waking up in the middle of the night, having made a highly technical discovery at the very instant that a Yale mathematician made the same discovery on the other side of the Atlantic. Our minds are often more receptive to emotional influences than they are to intellectual ones. Even in ordinary conversation, which usually has a good deal of emotional content behind it, *rapport* occurs that is by no means explicable in positivistic terms.

If we are so receptive at the unconscious level not only to the other ends of our planet but to the "collective unconscious" of our race, we may well be exposed to an unlimited range of psychic influences. At that level I think we are. Therein, indeed, lies much of the danger that people in bygone times expressed in terms of hobgoblins and the evil eye. For Christians, the power of Jesus Christ, as the Risen Lord, lies in his triumph over all such wild, troublesome, and often dangerous influences. At the invocation of his name they flee, instantly subdued. Now angels, being plainly "on his side," must surely be seen as partaking in that same spiritual power, for they are ambassadors of God. Then are we to look for them in that same dark maelstrom in which we find all kinds of commonplace psychic phenomena that whirl about disturbing and tormenting us? Is it there that we must examine angels along with these myriads of psychic vermin? Are angels, after all, really fit subjects for psychical research?

Yes and no. No, in the sense that if they exist at all they are not for sweeping up along with everything else we find in that cavernous backwater of our souls. Yes, because although they do not belong there, it might well be that thither they go to bring us the tidings of God. If, as Christian orthodoxy has always insisted, the manger was fit to receive the Incarnate Son of God, why should not the *id* be fit for his envoys to go in search of us? Not the *Ucs.* but the *Pcs.* (if we are to use Freudian terminology): the screen against which the angels' wings may with one flutter silence the brood of vipers and at the same time be heard by us?

If angels are such superior beings (and unless we take seriously the possibility that they are, what is the point of inquiring into them?) we may well listen for them and wait upon them there. For thither one might expect them to go as the parents of a prodigal son would go to the lowest pit of his despair, not to stay long with him there, of course, but to raise him up.

If, however, we venture further still, taking seriously the hypothesis at the heart of our study, that angels might be not only beings superior to us but beings who have progressed further in evolutionary development than we (as indeed the Mahayana concept of the bodhisattva more explicitly suggests), and are therefore to be deemed our suprahuman kith and kin, they can become for us infinitely more meaningful. They might then be anything from beings far beyond our capacity to apprehend to beings only a little higher than ourselves: beings who might be even in some cases men and women we have known and loved. In such cases the methods used in psychical research might be suitable for our investigation of the nature and purpose of their concern for us and our better understanding of the ways in which we put obstacles in the path of these envoys of God. If the methods used by psychical research could be so applied, they would do us more service than merely confirming the authenticity of the experience of making contact with deceased friends on "the other side."

Would that sort of research be contrary to the teachings of traditional Christian orthodoxy? I cannot see that it would. Attempts to disturb the spirits beyond the veil of death are indeed alien to the Christian faith and run counter to the ancient Catholic prayer for the dead that they may "rest in peace." For we cannot know from what important work or needful rest we might be disturbing them. To detect their presence when *they* are calling upon *us* would be very different.

17

ANGELS AND ANDROGYNS

. . . androgyny has become a general formula signifying autonomy, strength, wholeness; to say of a divinity that it is androgyne is as much as to say that it is the ultimate being, the ultimate reality.
—MIRCEA ELIADE, *Myths, Dreams, and Mysteries*

Are we to think of angels as sexless or androgynous? Before attempting to answer that question we must clarify the meaning and implications of androgyny.

First, we must dispel from our minds all analogies from human sexuality. These come naturally to us whenever sexuality is mentioned. We must not suppose, for instance, that androgyns would lack sexuality as we understand it; yet no less must we avoid imagining them as combining male and female sexuality as one might mix red and blue in order to get mauve. In the androgyn, sexuality as we understand it has been transcended. Although it is perfected (or restored to an original perfection), it is so far beyond our concepts of sexuality, even the noblest of them, that we cannot pretend to know what it would be. We could no more pretend to know that than we could pretend to know what a perfected intelligence would be or even a perfectly healthy body, since even the most brilliant of human minds has many limitations and even the healthiest of bodies is sure to have some imbalance or other and perhaps a few bruises. The very notion of androgyny as completeness or perfection of something that we know only in a divided state implies that human sexuality as we know it *is* imperfect in the

172

sense that it lacks something that ideally it should have. It is not a question of attaining a higher or finer quality of the sexuality we have. We may do that as human beings and most of us do, let us hope, as we mature, making the calmer years of maturity even more beautiful than the stormier years of our youth and investing us with a deeper sexuality than ever despite a decline in the urgency of desire. Androgyny, however, so surpasses all stages and gradations of the sexuality we know that its perfection is and must be beyond our imagining. At best we can imagine it only, as Paul says of all our present knowledge, "through a glass darkly." Nevertheless, opaque though our conception may be, we can in some way dimly conceive the meaning of it.

Second, if we are to think of angels as androgyns we must recognize that since angels are traditionally considered to be immortal, not subject as we are to death, they can have no need to reproduce themselves, so that their "sexuality" could not include this function. Yet we are not bound to accept that traditional view. If, for example, we are subject to rebirth (as is widely held in many of the great religions of the world and is more widely believed among Christians than we often suppose)[1] angels might be similarly subject to rebirth, although in their own, presumably very different, way. They would not die as we do, nor would they enter again and again into new wombs; nevertheless, they might pass through a process somehow analogous to ours. True, (as some theosophical writers teach) they may be on a different evolutionary path from ours, in which spiritual growth is accomplished in ways unlike those by which we advance in spiritual maturity, but if love is (as the writer of the first letter of John insists) the primary and essential attribute of God (I John 4:8), then even angels must advance by perfecting themselves in love, which we humans learn through the medium of our sexuality if we learn it at all. So the *principle* of their evolutionary movement would not be entirely different from ours.

Third, androgyny would seem, indeed, to imply a nature so different from ours that whatever corporeality these beings might have would make them in some very fundamental way alien from us. They might be able, for example, to pass through one another or coincide with one another, and that would be (would it not?) a kind of sexual embrace. After all, we recognize that plants have a sexuality, although it is very different from our own. Why might not there be higher modes of sexuality even more different from ours than ours are from those of trees and plants? For millions of sperm cells to be chasing a solitary ovum is certainly not the only possible way in which a species can be reproduced, nor is there any reason to suppose that it must be the highest or best way; but it is the way in which *human* reproduction is accomplished. There is no reason, however, why androgynous angels should not reproduce themselves, if they reproduce themselves at all, in some other way that at present we may not be able even to imagine. Or again, spiritual growth in an androgynous state might be attained, of course, without reproduction but in an embrace so complete as to constitute corporeal coincidence.

There is an interesting tendency in some literature to assign androgynous qualities to heroes and heroines. We miss the point of this literary device if we think of androgyny merely as sexual completeness. It is, both as a literary and as a religious archetype, much more complex. It symbolizes wholeness, perfection: the perfection of a primordial state of undividedness. Heroes must be more than men, yet assuredly they must be men; heroines must certainly be women, yet more than women. How is this to be done? A classic formula is to exaggerate the masculinity of the heroes and the femininity of the heroines, as Shakespeare does with Lady Macbeth and her husband, who become, in effect, divided androgyns. If we are to transcend humanity, whether in religious teaching or literary imagination, we cannot well escape the myth of the androgyn.

C. S. Lewis, in a fascinating essay entitled "The Mistake about Milton's Angels,"[2] suggests that Milton in *Paradise Lost* was "imprudent in raising a matter which invites" misunderstanding, namely, that in Milton the angels are all alluded to by masculine pronouns so that "we tend, half consciously," in view of what Henry More had called "the amorous propensities" of Milton's angels (*Paradise Lost*, VIII, 618–29), "to think that Milton is attributing to them a life of homosexual promiscuity." C. S. Lewis goes on to point out that since Milton's angels do not die they do not need to breed, so they are not sexed "in the human sense at all." Nevertheless, "there exists among these creatures, according to Milton, something that might be called trans-sexuality. The impulse of mutual love is expressed by the total interpenetration of two aerial bodies; 'total they mix' because they are ductile and homogeneous—they mix like wine and water, or rather like two wines. The idea escapes the sensuality sometimes cast in Milton's teeth because the desire for total union, the impossible desire as it is for human lovers, is not the same thing as a desire for pleasure. Pleasure can be obtained; total interpenetration cannot, and, if it could, would be the satisfaction of love itself rather than of appetite. As Lucretius points out, men seek (and find) pleasure, insofar as they lust: they seek (and cannot achieve) total union insofar as they are lovers."[3] Finally, he observes that no doubt "these angelic fusions, since angels are corporeal, are not without pleasure: but we must not imagine it after the pattern of our own specialized and rebellious senses. Milton's angels are what may be called Panorganic—'all heart they live, all head, all eye, all ear, all intellect, all sense' " (*Paradise Lost,* VI, 350).[4]

Lewis is indeed perceptive here. But is he perceptive enough? Do we not, despite the nature of our sexuality, have within us the capacity to transcend it even in this life insofar as we may mature so as to engage in a spiritual fusion where spirit and spirit entwine in a love which, rooted though it is in sexuality, leaps beyond into a realm unimpeded by our kind of corporeality? At least we do so well enough to understand what Lewis is talking about when he speaks of Milton's angels.

Milton, of course, was following an ancient tradition (call it Gnostic if you will) which the great Alexandrian school of Christian philosophy followed, according to which the universe is full of incarnate spirits who are corporeal although not as densely corporeal as we who plod around in our heavy flesh-and-bone bodies. They are seen only by clairvoyant eyes. So Milton's angels, in accordance with that ancient tradition, really do eat and excrete, although not in our crass way. They are not disembodied spirits; it is just that their embodiment is so much finer than ours that they might seem to us to be so.

Milton, who was extraordinarily learned, could not but be familiar with that ancient tradition in all its complex detail. Bodies may be organized, as we know well from modern biology, in many different ways. We, if we lose an arm or a leg, cannot grow another, but we know very well that within the animal kingdom are to be found other creatures who, when they lose a part of their bodies, can indeed do that. Teilhard de Chardin relates that as a little boy he was fascinated by the fact that he could have his hair cut with impunity. His hair and his nails would grow again; his fingers and toes and head would not. So there is no reason why angels' bodies should be *totally* different from ours. Christians who are accustomed to accept the Gospel which records that Jesus, after his resurrection, could walk through doors yet also ate food, need not be unduly scandalized by the idea of androgynous angels who, though they may be able to zoom from one planet to another in a fraction of a second, may eat and excrete in their own way and even love through total interpenetration.

But if they do this, then they and their androgynous nature, different though it be from ours, need not be accounted totally different. Our human nature, with its half-bestial, half-angelic sexuality, might provide at least a pointer to a suprahuman state toward which we might be capable of moving. After all, we are extremely different from worms, yet no more than extremely different. The difference is not total. We recognize too that there are different kinds of love even in human experience. Again, the differences may be extreme, yet no more than extreme.

As all biblical scholars well know, several words are used to express "love" in Greek, each representing a different kind of love. *Erōs* is the one used for love in the sense of desire for something. Although commonly associated with sexual desire, it may refer to any kind of desire. It is a force drawing the lover to that which he loves, whatever it may be. Beyond *erōs,* however, is another sort of love, which in Greek is called *philia,* friendship. This word is a biblical one, found in both the Old Testament and the New. Aristotle saw *philia* as the richest capacity of the human spirit: the capacity for friendship. It may be associated with *erōs,* but it transcends it. Finally there is *agapē,* a term used in the New Testament for the love of God for man, of man for God: the love that is infused in the Church by the action of the Holy Spirit. It is a love that transcends even *philia* and is the characteristic disposition of the angels. Although rooted in their intellectual nature, *agapē* is not a product of it. It springs from God. To the extent that we develop our spiritual capacities we, too, can share in it and attain through it the special kind of intuitive knowledge that the angels so much more fully enjoy and use in the exercise of their missions.

The three kinds of love are indeed related to one another in the sense that *erōs,* for example, is not so much a rival to *agapē* as its groping and ineffective imitator. Erotic love is groping after agapistic love in the sense in which creatures at the lower levels of evolutionary development are groping toward consciousness but may need millions of years to find their way to it; the goal is not reached automatically but, on the contrary, requires a new turn in evolutionary development: an inturning to which, so far, the organism is unaccustomed. So *agapē* does not emerge naturally or spontaneously from eros as a tulip from the bulb we plant in the garden. It requires a special kind of "leap" or "turning." Christians traditionally have seen this as the work of the Holy Spirit acting in the community that is the Church, initiated by the grace of God.

But if angels, being so far beyond even the finest and noblest of men and women, have so long ago made this "leap" or "turning" and attained that *agapē* to such a superlative degree, how can they fall so quickly and so far? In most schemes of spiritual evolution, set-backs do occur. One may sometimes take one step forward, then two back. As in scientific discovery one may have a period of rapid progress followed by stagnation, so in spiritual development I may make a quantum leap followed by what the writers on ascetic theology call a time of torpor or weariness *(accidie)*. But neither do scientists suddenly fall back overnight to pre-Copernican astronomy or Aristotelian medicine nor does a great master of the spiritual life suddenly become a vulgar oaf. Setbacks are not like that. How then did the notion ever arise, as it did in the Judeo-Christian heritage, that Satan and his minions fell like lightning from the highest heaven to the lowest hell?

Christian orthodoxy was able to entertain such a concept in working with a schema in which all had been well in heaven and on earth: a time when the angels were totally unrebellious and Adam and Eve walked naked together in the Garden of Eden, where also the lion lay down at peace with the lamb. In such a scenario there was perhaps a sort of "cultural androgyny": a state in which nothing of the order of sexual lust could disturb the equanimity of God's creation. Nor did it, according to orthodox Christian teaching. What did the mischief was a far greater and more frightening evil: pride. So fundamental an evil is pride that it is at the root of all others. In the fully androgynous state, the angels are beyond the carnal temptations of men and women, which at worst merely hinder spiritual advancement; but their androgyny does not by any means place them beyond pride, an infinitely more damaging peril. Dante followed sound medieval teaching when he made pride the basic sin to be eradicated first before the steep ascent up the purgatorial mountain could begin. So radical is it that it not only remains a danger at the androgynous level of the angels; it lies behind and affects all sin. So it was the cause of Lucifer's fall, even at his level, the highest any creature had attained. According to Milton it was behind the downfall of Eve. The androgynous Satan, in the form of a serpent in the Garden of Eden, did not accomplish the fall of humanity by anything so simple and straightforward as an aphrodisiac apple, which at worst could have merely retarded humankind in its pilgrimage. No, according to Milton, he was more cunning; he titillated Eve's pride. First he assures her that all living things are admiring her beauty (IX, 532–41); next he makes her feel deprived, with only Adam to see her. She is persuaded at length that God wants to keep her in subjection, while she deserves to be lifted up. Still, she vacillates. This fruit that is forbidden by God might indeed be lethal. The serpent says it will make her divine, a goddess. At first she is inclined to keep the fruit to herself and so dominate Adam. Then, poisoned by pride, she remembers that there is risk in the adventure. She may die. She gives Adam the fruit so that, if she dies, Adam will die with her. Against the temptation of an androgynous angel neither Adam nor Eve could hope to win.

Milton could make this schema work even with a traditional theology of the Fall. In an evolutionary schema, with androgyny as an attainment of rather than a bestowal on the higher beings we call angels, it works even better. For here it means that I persuade myself that I can achieve advancement without effort, either because I am so favored by the gods or simply because of my natural right to it. In such a mood of pride I refuse to recognize how long and arduous is the path of spiritual advancement. I am in a hurry because I think of it as a trophy to be won, not as a moral achievement. Such a disposition poisons my soul at its very roots. Beside it, sins such as gluttony or avarice or sexual lust become secondary. They merely hinder my progress; they do not stop me in my tracks as does pride. Envy is a close runner-up to pride, being so much associated with it, but pride is the root of all the evils we create in ourselves and in the world around us. It works, moreover, in very devious ways, as Milton so skillfully shows. The pride of boastful arrogance may be much less noxious than that in which one disguises one's own pride to the world and even to oneself.

Androgynous angels, while they could love more deeply and completely than we, could also fall farther than we, for they would have farther to fall. Hence the notion of the horrific character of a diabolical will and the hideous nature of the intrigue in which it will engage: a concept that Lewis, once again, exploits so vividly in his ingenious little work, *The Screwtape Letters,* which demonstrates how subtle diabolical agencies are and what an easy prey we would be for them were it not for the good agencies that know, as we cannot, how to match and overcome them. For while androgyny, which I am positing as the state of sexual completeness proper to an angel, is lofty beyond our imagining, it is in its corrupted form unimaginably vile. Human sexuality, lovely as it is in its purity, turns sour and filthy when it is corrupted. What then must be the corrupted state of perfected sexuality, of androgyny? Not all the gruesome imagery the medieval writers and artists used to depict Satan and his legions could do justice to its vileness, while even the most morbidly sick contemporary cinematographic exercises in sex-and-violence would be a macabre understatement of the turpitude of an androgyn gone wrong.

So perhaps the notion of Satan and his diabolical legions, far from being the quaint bygone superstition that many take it to be, is worth taking much more seriously. For the higher we climb the farther we have to fall, and unless we are content to suppose that we have come all this way from Lucy and her peers and have now reached the end of our evolutionary journey, we cannot ignore the probability that higher intelligences than we could create even a worse blight than we have created in our own little world. Milton's genius lies in no small measure in his vivid poetic portrayal of that fundamental moral fact. Since moral values do not even arise except in triumph over evil, war in heaven is even more fearsome than war on earth. When we fail to appreciate that, the Christian claim that Christ has vanquished evil, destroying it at its very root, is meaningless.

18

WHY ANGELS?

Angels are men of a superior kind;
Angels are men in lighter habit clad.
EDWARD YOUNG, *Night Thoughts*

his chapter is more especially for those whose religious thought has been moulded primarily by the Bible and the Reformation heritage.

Why angels? Is not God sufficient?

The second of these two questions is one that comes naturally to those in whose ears echo the words that Saint Paul tells us he received from Christ: "My grace is sufficient for thee" (II Corinthians 12:9). If God's grace, given me through Christ, is sufficient for me, why do I need angels?

No Christian asking such a question would necessarily be denying the reality of the phenomenon called "angel." He or she would not be saying that angels are fictions except as the manifestation of something arising from the superego in the human psyche. He would be saying, rather, that "angel" is simply a poetic way of talking of the divine presence. We all know that in art angels are depicted with pretty wings and other appurtenances and of course we all recognize that these are artistic metaphors, so why not consider the notion of angels to be itself a metaphor for God's presence? Why encumber us with the notion of another order of beings?

The point seems at first well taken, at any rate by those of us who wish to uphold, as I do, the sovereignty of God. Nevertheless, the

180

question is really of the same order as the question "Does God exist?" As existence is an inadequate category for God, so also is "sufficiency." To say that God is sufficient is somewhat like saying that two parents were sufficient for my having been born. Of course they were sufficient, but they were much more: they were all that could possibly ever be needed, in our system of human reproduction, for my birth physically to have taken place. I would not have been any better off with an extra parent. So we have to say that God is beyond the category of sufficiency as he is beyond the category of existence.

With that in mind we may now proceed with the first question, the one that is the title of this chapter: Why angels? If we are to recognize God and talk about him at all we must recognize that his creativity is infinite and his love is always flowing with a magnanimity beyond our imagining. Why, then, should he need to use intermediaries? Does he need to employ agents to carry his messages as we employ the United Parcel Service? Is his voice so weak that he needs to use, as sometimes we must, a public address system? Of course such notions are ludicrous. Why, then, angels? Are not they indeed just names for the manifestation of God's presence?

Those in the Reformation heritage will most easily see the force of the question. For one of the battle cries of the Reformation was against the invocation of saints. Why should we pray to this or that saint when we have free access to God? If God deigns to answer our prayer at all or deems it expedient so to do, he will do so by his own fiat, his own decree. Certainly he will not be more likely to answer my prayer because I have engaged a heavenly advocate more saintly than I to whom he might more readily listen. Since he knows all and listens to all and is ever-ready to forgive the penitent, he will hear my pleadings as readily, if not more readily, if I earnestly implore him directly and secretly in my own heart. He will not listen to me any better if I go through influential celestial channels. That might be the best way to approach an earthly power-broker; but God is not any kind of power broker. Our using such methods might indeed vitiate our approach to God. Would a loving father be pleased if his prodigal son approached him through an attorney? Would a loving father use an attorney to talk to his prodigal son if he could talk to him directly, as God can? So once again: Why angels? May not we simply write them off as a mytho-poeic way of expressing the divine presence as we encounter it?

At the time of the Reformation these questions must have had an immensely compelling force. For one could still think in terms of God's having made each species separately, with man at the end of the act of creation, as its pinnacle and completion. What is so impressive about the treatment of angels in Thomas Aquinas is that even without an evolutionary understanding of the universe he perceived a reason why angels are needed in the hierarchy of being. Thomas was never more perceptive than he was in providing for angels as the next step in the order of being beyond man. True, he found the idea in Scripture and took it (as he took all Scripture) as revealed truth: the disclosure of God to man concerning his nature and his will for humankind. Thomas saw that Scripture may and often does teach *per similitudinem,* that is, by metaphors and other figures of speech. He discusses this at the beginning of his greatest work, before even broaching the question of the Being of God.[1] So when it came to angels, much later on, he might very well have treated them as figurative: a way of talking about the presence of God as the prophets felt it and as the people of God have found it in the course of their history. On the contrary, however, he took angels very seriously, recognizing them as ontologically distinct in a hierarchy of being.

We might usefully compare, moreover, Thomas's treatment of angels with his treatment of the notion of creation in time. The latter doctrine, he says, comes only through divine revelation; it cannot be proved "demonstratively" by rational argument.[2] (His reasons for supposing this happen to have been wrong, but that is irrelevant here.) When it comes to angels, however, he makes no such disclaimer. Although it is through Scripture that we come to learn of angels as such, reason would lead us to some such conclusion in any case. He argues that there must be some incorporeal creatures because, since intellect is above sense, there must be some creatures who are incorporeal and therefore comprehensible by the intellect alone.[3] The perfection of the universe, he argues, "requires the existence of an incorporeal creature."[4] Again, his reasons we would disavow; but he saw, within the intellectual framework of his day and in the light of his principal task, which was the reconciliation of Aristotle (science) with Scripture (religion), why it makes sense to suppose that man cannot be the "ultimate" in creation and that there must be creatures ontologically superior to him.

In the intellectual climate of today we know both that we have had an evolutionary past and that the entire universe works, as far as we can tell, on an evolutionary principle, which in modern Judaeo-Christian language we have been calling "God's way of doing things." The hypothesis that humankind has an evolutionary future now seems as plausible as the hypothesis that the tree I planted five years ago and that has been doing well so far will continue to grow during the next five. It is not certain; it might be overtaken by blight; but everything in experience and local knowledge points to its happening as I expect.

Now when we ask: Why angels? our answer can be a sort of updated Thomist one. That is, a Christian or Jew may go on saying that the existence of angels as ontological entities is a biblical datum, given to us as the revelation or disclosure of God; but he or she may also add that the notion is not only a revelatory "given" but is also, from what we know about space and the evolutionary process, possible or even probable. Angels could be not incorporeal, but with embodiments so much finer than our own as to make them seem *poetically* incorporeal by comparison, in the sense in which a cloud seems poetically incorporeal alongside a mountain, or a rainbow behind a forest of sequoias. More importantly, angels can now be conceived as not merely constituting a possibility but as representing an order of being whose existence is to be expected in view of the magnitude and complexity of the universe, on the one hand, and on the other, of the stupendous time-range we must envision whenever we think of evolutionary developments. When the psalmist sings to Yahweh that

> To you, a thousand years are a single day,
> a yesterday now over, an hour of the night,[5]

he can now be seen to have understated the case. The three million years or so between Lucy and us are truly miniscule in comparison with the age of even our own obscure little nook of the galaxy, the Milky Way, to say nothing of the universe beyond. The complexity of man, astounding as it is, could be amoeba-like in comparison to higher forms of life of which we have as yet no empirical knowledge.

So much for scientific possibilities. But from a theological standpoint how are we to respond to the question: Why angels?

If we posit God as Creator (as Christianity and other religions do) and also recognize the evolutionary character of the creative process, it is difficult, if not impossible, to suppose that humanity represents the endpoint in the process. Even if the Bible had nothing to say about angels, and the Church throughout the ages had been silent on the subject, it would still be difficult for any thoughtful and imaginative person to be content with the notion that we are the best that God can do. Humanity may indeed have far to go before any radical modification takes place, but if we have taken so long to get to where we are it seems almost unintelligible to suggest that this is where we stop. Such a view would imply, theologically, that the entire universe was created with humanity as its goal. That is the sort of anthropocentrism that I have already proposed to dismiss, along with geocentrism, as outmoded. The glory of man is in no way diminished by such a dismissal. On the contrary, humanity is a beacon pointing to the creative work in progress and a token of the spirituality it portends.

The adaptability of man has brought him to where he is, with all its pitfalls and with all its potentialities. He could still fail; but such is the amazing diversity of *homo sapiens* that although some types might conceivably wither, decay, and eventually become extinct, others will survive. Moreover, if Christian faith is right in believing in resurrection of one kind or another through the power of Christ, then what can this mean but that those who attain this resurrected state will be transmogrified, becoming the "new man," the "new being."

The theme of a "remnant" runs all the way through the biblical story and is prominent in prophetic utterances. The term "remnant" was originally a neutral one meaning simply that which remains after conquest. From this was developed the theological idea of the People of God who, after conquest, survive as an act of the righteous judgment of Yahweh and who are bearers, therefore, of his promise. Nevertheless, the prophets frequently warn the people of Israel that the promise is conditional upon their fidelity to Yahweh and their observance of the righteous conduct he expects. Otherwise the remnant itself shall be purged or even destroyed (Jeremiah 6:9; 8:3; 15:9; 24:8; Ezekiel 5:10; Isaiah 10:22). Yet such threats serve also to exhibit the nature and the glory of the promise. The remnant is the locus of God's redeeming action. It is there that he has conferred the opportunity for his people to grow and to blossom. The survival of the remnant is, moreover, itself a token of the fidelity of God toward his people. He has saved his remnant from destruction and is calling them to a still greater destiny. Christians interpreted this ancient notion of a remnant as having been fulfilled in the shaping of the New Israel, the Church, the *ekklēsia* or assembly of the faithful.

Of course neither Jews nor Christians necessarily interpreted this notion in terms of development and growth such as I am suggesting here. But then, neither did the recipients of the biblical promise necessarily interpret it in messianic terms. Jews certainly did not interpret it in terms of what Christians eventually took to be the messianic nature of God's purpose, nor could Christians generally have envisioned the kind of purpose I am proposing here. But then, once again, neither could Christians in the past have generally been equipped to interpret the original Christian vision of the Coming of the Kingdom in the evolutionary light that is now possible for us, with the kind of growth and development, social and individual, that this implies.

Angels, therefore, remained curiously detached from the process of the Coming of the Kingdom of God. Humanity was deeply involved in it; indeed, Christ's entire birth, life, passion, death, and resurrection had been seen as focused on humanity to the exclusion of all else, including the entire range of subhuman life, whose presence was a mystery except insofar as it could be understood in terms of service to man. (Horses, camels, and other beasts of burden served man's transportation needs, sheep his need for warm clothing, while fish, birds, and various mammals served his need for food.) In this highly anthropocentric understanding of God's purposes, angels were an anomaly. They were creatures of God of course no less than we; yet they seemed outside the scope of his central plan of action for creation. They existed to serve him and that service might include missions to man who, *faute de mieux,* seemed the focus and goal of the entire process of creation, which had begun in or with time itself and which would cease, as obviously must any enterprise, on the completion of the process and the attainment of the end for which the enterprise was begun.

Such a model simply will not work for us, unless we blind ourselves to everything that we know about the universe so far. Besides, even if we do care to blind ourselves, this model is too meager, too impoverished an interpretation of what must be the nature of the Kingdom of God. That angels do not fit into it may be an intellectual embarrassment, but if so it is only one among a far wider range of problems. As soon as we take account of other stages of evolution (both those behind us and those ahead) and of other possible lines of evolution going on either around us or in remote reaches of the universe, angels not only fit into the traditional talk of the Coming of the Kingdom of God; they are what we would expect.

Alice Meynell, who died in 1922, hinted at the scenario that has since been so much more forcefully imposed upon thinking people. In her beautiful poem entitled *Christ in the Universe,* she wrote of Christ:

> Nor, in our little day,
> May his devices with the heavens be guessed;
> His pilgrimage to thread the Milky Way,
> Or his bestowals there be manifest.
>
> But in the eternities
> Doubtless we shall compare together, hear
> A million alien gospels, in what guise
> He trod the Pleiades, the Lyre, the Bear.[6]

Such a vision certainly no more "proves" the existence of angels than it "proves" the existence of extraterrestrials of any kind; but if, as seems so very likely, man is not the sole focus of the creative process, then Christians must see the entire concept of the Cosmic Christ with a grander sweep than ever before and in a perspective within which angels, by whatever name they might be called, would be theologically inescapable. The Council of Chalcedon, in 451 CE, determined that Christ is True God and True Man. We now have to take account of possibilities such as the hypothetical case of an inhabited Mars, where Christ's being True Man would be as irrelevant to Martians as would be a decree by a General Council on our planet Earth that he is True God and True Martian. With our sights so changed, angels, like evolution itself, can be seen as, to say the least, a most likely aspect of "God's way of doing things."

33. MICHAEL SLAYING THE DRAGON.

Icon, probably Coptic. Byzantine Museum, Athens. Michael's slaying of the dragon is not a once-for-all event. It occurs every time a soul, in the course of strife within, achieves victory over evil.

34. THREE ANGELS;
    HELLENISTIC, ISLAMIC, AND
    CHRISTIAN.
    The Hellenistic angel is in
    the form of a detail of
    Hebe from an antique vase
    painting; the Islamic one is
    from a detail of a Mughal
    miniature; the Christian one
    is from a detail of the
    Annunciation by Melozzo
    da Forli (1438–1494) in the
    Uffizi, Florence.

35. ANGELS HOVER OVER ADAM AND EVE.
William Blake (1757–1827), *Adam and Eve Sleeping.* Watercolor.
Museum of Fine Arts, Boston.

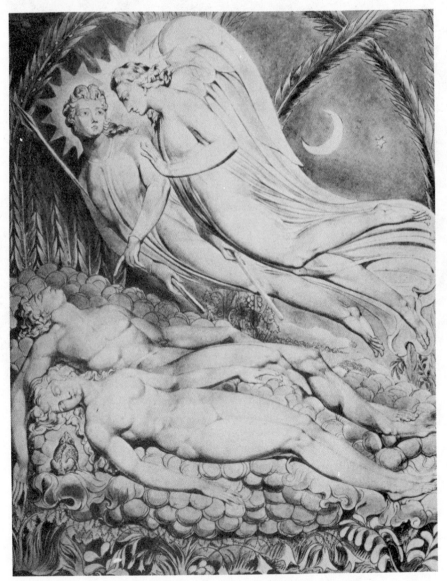

36. DANIEL WITH LIONS AND GUARDIAN ANGELS.
From an 8th century Commentary on the Apocalypse by Beatus, a
Spanish monk. British Museum.

37. GABRIEL IN SERENITY.
Jan and Hubert van Eyck (1370–1426, 1395–1441), detail from
the altarpiece at Ghent.

38. ANGELS MAKE MUSIC.
Simone Marmion (c. 1425–1489), detail from *Choir of Angels*. An
example of the frequently found motif of angels playing musical
instruments.

39. ISIS AS A WINGED ANGEL.
The ancient Egyptian goddess Isis is here depicted as an angel
enfolding her devotees in sleep.

40. AN ORTHODOX MICHAEL.
In this 16th century Russian icon, Michael is seen in a triumphal form
favored in some Eastern Orthodox representations: a benign ruler
rather than a messenger.

19

ANGELS AND EVOLUTION

O everlasting God, who has ordained and constituted the ministries
of angels and men in a wonderful order: Mercifully grant that, as thy
holy angels always serve and worship thee in heaven, so by thy
appointment they may help and defend us on earth; through Jesus
Christ our Lord, who liveth and reigneth with thee and the Holy
Spirit, one God for ever and ever.

Book of Common Prayer, 1979
(TRADITIONAL COLLECTS), P. 200

In the course of this study of
angels I have repeatedly pleaded for taking them seriously. But in
what way, precisely, is the seriousness to be taken?

Whatever our answer to that question is to be, it will depend on
the way in which we take God seriously. As is our attitude to God,
so will be our attitude to the concept of angels.

Suppose, for example, that the universe has no source or spring
or ground in anything that could be regarded as corresponding in
any way to the Being of God as we encounter that Being in the
biblical heritage and elsewhere in the great religions of the world.
Suppose that the universe simply *is* and needs no such explanatory
focus, no such creative principle that might be identifiable with
God. That would not necessarily mean that we should no longer
use the term "God." We might use it, for instance, to represent any
important psychological archetype: a father-image or mother-im-
age, for example. We talk freely about Santa Claus all our lives,
although few of us have believed in his existence since we attained
the age of five.

195

Not only indeed do we talk of him; we jealously guard the idea of Santa Claus and of what he stands for in the human spirit and in human society. We deplore and even ridicule any who, like Scrooge, denigrate the idea, although no one believes he exists otherwise than as a creation of the human mind to represent a certain spirit of generosity and warmth that we all see as an ideal condition of the human psyche. He is a symbol of the human spirit at its best.

Moreover, having established Santa Claus as an important symbolic functionary, we have no difficulty in going on to provide him with a suitable entourage and various accoutrements proper to his function. He has a team of "helpers." We even name them. He has reindeer for transportation. Even his dress and facial appearance are rigorously prescribed by the laws of folklore. A clean-shaven Santa is unthinkable. Even a Van Dyke beard would be quite unacceptable, for such a Santa would not be a "real" Santa, although no Santa Claus exists except in the human imagination. The members of his entourage must also conform to certain traditional requirements. A little latitude may be permitted here and there, but the main lines are carefully drawn and deviations from them are forbidden.

If, then, our concept of God is constructed along similar lines, his entourage will function similarly. Angels, sprites, gnomes, elves, imps, and all the rest of the folklore populace will have their appointed places. I recall that as a little boy I was taken to a pantomime in which the fairy godmother happened to be a rather portly and buxom woman who waved her wand with the energy and panache of a symphony conductor. I protested (very justifiably, I think) that she was not a "real" fairy godmother, although by that time I had not the slightest belief in the existence of such entities. I knew, however, what was to be expected of a fairy godmother and I was no more about to accept the lady in question than I would have accepted a benign dragon or a six-foot elf. A fairy godmother is dainty and petite, almost as a unicorn has by definition one horn, and all this although neither unicorns nor dragons nor fairy godmothers exist.

So, thinking along such lines, we should have no difficulty in fitting angels into the furnishings of our minds. We shall go on expecting them to be properly attired with wings as we shall go on expecting their diabolical counterparts to have the horns and tails proper to their state. We may even feel that something is far wrong with the idea of a devil wearing a halo as illustrated in this book (Fig. 32), for it does not accord with the "protocol" of folklore, although we would laugh at the notion of the existence of devils as entities independent of our minds.

Our attitude to angels, then, would be entirely determined by our initial anthropocentric presupposition: that man constitutes the highest order of intelligence and moral awareness in the universe, and that any entity higher than ourselves must therefore be solely a construct of our minds, a father figure, mother figure, big brother figure, baby figure, or what you will.

If, however, we change the entire scenario by positing that the universe does have its spring, its source, its ground, in the Being of God (by whatever name the spring of the universe be called), several radically different consequences follow. One of them is that even without our knowing about an evolutionary principle in the universe (as was the case until comparatively recent times), the notion that humanity is the best that such an almighty Creator could do seems at best unimaginative and narrow-minded and at worst perverse. Our forefathers, although they knew so little by our standards of the magnitude of the universe, had only to look around them and see dogs and cats, monkeys and sparrows, on the one hand, and then, on the other hand, "the starry heavens above" in order to doubt that man, for all his grandeur and obvious mental superiority, can represent the highest achievement possible for him who has created such wonders.

When, for complex historical reasons, the idea of beings higher than man was expressed in biblical literature and the Judaeo-Christian tradition in the form of angels, it was easy to fit them into the general understanding of God's creative activity. True, the way in which creation would have been understood based on a literal interpretation of Genesis would cause many people to think of it as instantaneous. According to the first chapter of Genesis, God simply decreed that light should come into existence where only darkness had been. He uttered the *fiat* "Let there be light" and light appeared. So, many would suppose that sheep and goats and dogs and cats and each kind of bird and fish would likewise have been created spontaneously, with a similarly instantaneous directive, although a closer reading of Genesis I (as we saw earlier) reveals even there a process that takes time and energy such that at the end even God takes a rest, a *šabbat*.

Since that seemed to many the way in which creation was

accomplished, what reason could there be not to suppose that angels were created in the same way, as a separate order of being, closer to the Being of God and with capacities beyond those of even the best of us? The fact that to a believer in God today our forefathers were indubitably mistaken about the way in which God's creative act is conducted is of no great importance. Our forefathers were mistaken in many ways about the way in which things work. They were mistaken about the behavior of the sun and the planets and a great deal else, but they were right at least in thinking of them as really existing, rather than being concoctions of the human mind. We still agree with them about that.

The important difference we have to consider, then, is not how things work or how individuals or crowds tend to behave. The important difference is whether we are talking of what exists solely in the human mind or of what exists independently of it. If we take God seriously as the source of the universe and attribute to him qualities such as care and concern and love for his creation, then (along with our similarly believing forefathers) we should not find difficult the notion that beings higher than ourselves exist somewhere in this vast and multidimensional universe.

Indeed, unless we are pig-unimaginative and peasant-parochial in our thinking, we can hardly remain so insular as to be content with the notion that humanity is the best that such a Creator God can do. Were we so intellectually insular, we could not know the nature of humanity itself. "What should they know of England who only England know?" wrote Rudyard Kipling. Much the same could be said, by paraphrase, of those who do not understand the nature and genius of their own language, English, because they know none of the other languages that have contributed so much to its beauty, its nature, and its history: "What should they know of English, who only English know?" In the same vein we may well go on to a further paraphrase: "What should they know of humanity who only humans know?" For we really cannot understand ourselves or the role of humanity in the evolution of the universe till we at least envision the possibility of other and higher forms of life that God has placed elsewhere or has in the making.

I would go so far as to suggest that even if there were no mention of angels in the Bible and nothing about them in the long and complex tradition celebrated in literature, a sincere believer in God as the Creator of the universe would nowadays be compelled to make some sort of hypothesis about beings more advanced than we and therefore more attuned than most of us to the will and purposes of our Creator. That being so, to find that such beings are frequently mentioned in the sacred literature we have inherited should come as no surprise. That the idea of angels has obvious precursors in human thought, precursors of a more primitive, not to say frivolous kind, should not cloud our vision to what seems to me the extreme likelihood that such superior beings do exist.

Scientists no less than others often make mistakes about how things *work*. Even so great a scientist as Newton, who was also a religious man, accounted for the tangential velocities of the planets that prevent their falling into the sun by supposing that they had been initially hurled by God's hand and that what happened after the hurling is to be accounted for by the law of gravitation. But Newton's erroneous supposition is erroneous only about how things work in the universe (and it was less erroneous even on that than had been the theories of most of his predecessors); it does not affect the facts that these theories had been trying to explain. Such theories do nothing to warrant our belief in either the existence or the non-existence of God, and no theory of such a kind is likely ever to do so. What we can do is to clarify in our minds the difference between, for example, the view that since there is nothing higher in evolution than humanity, all the thoughts of man about something higher must spring from somewhere within his restless imagination, and the view that, given that evolution is a fundamental principle of all that we know about the universe, and that humanity has been in process for what is by cosmic standards only a short time, the probability of our being the highest form of evolutionary development, surpassed and surpassable by none, is singularly small. So small is it that even if I did *not* believe in God as the Creator of the universe (as I do believe) I should still find highly unlikely the notion that the summit of evolutionary development is to be found in man.

I have no dramatic encounter to relate of any angelic vision. Yet all through my life, from my first memories, which are very early and very vivid (desultory from just before my second birthday but copious from my third onwards), I have been aware of direction coming to me from a source beyond myself and often contrary both to my own personal inclinations and to the instincts I inherited from the past and acquired from my contemporaries.

At first I could discern no pattern in them and since I happen to be by nature inclined to appreciate orderliness and to enjoy rationality, I tended to resist or ignore such direction whenever it seemed offensive to the natural bent of my temperament. Only very slowly did I come to perceive, in these insistent whisperings from beyond, a superlatively subtle wisdom far beyond my own.

Even as a child I always felt more or less uncomfortable with the concept of angels. Even today a sense of absurdity still lingers in my mind at the very sound of the word, which to me carries such strong overtones of sentimental humbug. Yet what a reality is called matters little. In my boyhood we called Planet Earth "the world" and I do not see that it has changed as a result of our adopting more fashionable terminology. So I am not much interested in the name we are to give to what are traditionally called angels. My interest lies in the question of the possibility of their independent reality.

While still in my teens I was introduced to both Freud and Jung by an intelligent relative who had been captivated by the latter's thought. I read them avidly insofar as I could understand them at the time and was fascinated by them. Then quite suddenly I was seized with the feeling that not only were they not answering the questions to which I wanted answers; they were not even dealing with them. Instead of telling me about, say, chemistry or language or religion, they were theorizing from clinical experience with neurotic patients about what happens in my mind when I think about chemistry or language or religion and even why I ever get to thinking about them in the first place. It was as though, while I was trying to use my eyes to learn how better to appreciate art and my ears similarly for music, they were lecturing me on ophthalmology and otology, and more particularly on pathological aspects of these subjects. It was not that I was uninterested. I have ever since been interested in any psychological theories I have heard about or read. It is just that in view of the brevity of life one must have priorities and it has never seemed to me that I ought to place a study of such theories very high on my list.

In early childhood I had had an intense (some might say pathological) fascination for folklore stories. I read everything I could lay my hands on, comparing Scandinavian ones with Greek, the Arabian Nights with Hans Andersen, and even composing some of my own. I am certain that it never once occurred to me to take any of the mythological figures seriously. They were collector's items for the realm of my imagination and I happened to be extremely avaricious in such matters. My almost fanatical preoccupation with that private world of my imagination accustomed me to taking any kind of imaginative entity in my stride, from angels to dragons, from ogres to pixies. Far from diminishing my interest in realities outside that private world, however, it seemed to increase it.

My reason for having inflicted on my readers these last few autobiographical paragraphs is, I hope, now clear. I wish to dispel any lingering notion that I am inclined to ignore the psychological circumstances that lead people to think in terms of angels or indeed of anything else. Of course there are psychological reasons for everything. There are psychological reasons, I presume, for our having generally adopted the so-called Arabic numerals rather than, say, the Roman ones; but such psychological circumstances have no bearing upon mathematics. Nor do our dreams of flying out the window at night over the rooftops have any bearing upon the reality or unreality of angels.

In writing this book on angels I have had no brief for either the prosecution or the defense. My purpose has been, rather, to call attention to a possibility that seems to me to have been widely overlooked, largely because we have not yet accustomed ourselves to the full implications of the evolutionary principle to be found wherever we look in the universe. Is it entirely impossible, then, that the angel of the Lord who spoke to Abraham when he was about to offer up his son Isaac (Genesis 22:11–18) as a human sacrifice was a real entity belonging to a higher stage of evolutionary development? We may well doubt it. Most educated people do. But then some biblical scholars in the recent past were inclined to view Abraham himself as fictitious figure, although few today, if any, would carry historical skepticism so far.

Suppose now, however, that clear evidence had been found, either from extraterrestrial signals or parapsychological data, satisfying most educated people of the existence of such superhuman entities whom we might as well call angels, since that is a traditional and convenient term, and suppose further that we had similarly clear evidence of their benevolence and habitual helpfulness toward us. What difference might it be expected to make to our attitudes and our thinking?

To the extent that we fully absorbed its implications, this information would not necessarily incline more people toward belief in God, but it would radically affect our attitude to and understanding of man. No longer could we think in such parochial terms or with such blatant arrogance about humanity. No longer could we think of man either along traditional "religious" lines as God's ultimate creative achievement or along traditional "non-religious" lines as our own "do-it-yourself" accomplishment and one which, never having been part of any more general purpose but purely an exercise in survival, is therefore in the nature of the case precarious, since our own skill in survival might easily boomerang, turning our self-development into self-destruction as might a clever chemist who, having invented an undetectable poison for murdering one's enemies with impunity, inadvertently drinks it himself.

If my book has succeeded in so broadening the perspective of any of my readers, it will have succeeded in its main purpose. If in addition to that it has at least furnished others with helpful information and even here and there pleasant entertainment, I shall be glad to have provided such services as a bonus.

NOTES

INTRODUCTION

1. For an exposition of the nature of religious faith, see my article "Doubt and Belief" in *The Encyclopaedia of Religion* (New York: The Macmillan Company, 1987).

CHAPTER 2—ANGELS IN CATHOLIC TRADITION

1. This is all the more remarkable in view of the fact that Pope John Paul II frequently mentions angels; e.g., he devoted three of his series of addresses at his weekly audiences in St. Peter's Square, Rome, on July 9, 23, and 30, 1986, to the subject. Indeed, Father Raymond Panikkar, author of *The Unknown Christ in Hinduism*, wrote in a letter to *The Tablet* (October 18, 1986): "Many Catholics, especially the intellectuals, have felt a sort of embarrassment at the frequent mention by Pope John Paul II of angels and demons. But I for one am in sympathy with him."

2. *Honoramus eos [angelos] caritate, non servitute.* By *servitus* (slavery) Augustine here intends the total allegiance due by a slave to a master. A formal distinction was developed in Catholic thought to exhibit the radical nature of the difference between the worship of God, to whom alone such worship is due, and the reverence given to angels and saints: the former is *latria,* the latter *doulia.* Even the special devotion due to Mary is only *hyperdoulia* and therefore qualitatively different from *latria.*

3. To the best of my knowledge, no such text from any medieval schoolman has ever been found. The nearest that I know about is in an anonymous fourteenth-century mystical treatise, *Swester Katrei,* which refers to a thousand souls in heaven sitting on the point of a needle. In Le Puy, a town in the Haute-Loire, some 90 miles southwest of Lyon, is a steep and sharp volcanic cone known as L'Aiguille ("The Needle") on which was built a chapel dedicated to Michael. During the Middle Ages attempts were made to build chapels to the other archangels, but they all collapsed. Accordig to local tradition there was a short-lived university in the town and it was there that theological disputations arose on the question, "How many angels can stand atop a needle?" I am indebted to my friend Fr. Cyril Molnar for this information and have not so far examined the merits of the claim. But also see Chapter 8, note 17.

CHAPTER 3—ANGELS IN THE BIBLE

1. For a detailed exposition of Islamic teaching on angels, see the long article, "Malā'ika" (angels) in *The Encyclopaedia of Islam* (Leiden: E. J. Brill, 1936).

CHAPTER 4—GOOD AND EVIL AGENCIES IN BIBLICAL AND GNOSTIC LITERATURE

1. Enoch is a heterogeneous collection of Jewish writings dating from the last two centuries BCE

2. *Duo eisin aggeloi meta tou anthrōpou, eis tē dikaiosunēs kai eis tēs ponērias.*

3. *Unaquaeque etiam anima, dum in corpus mittitur, angelo committitur* (*Elucidarium*, II, 31).

4. By this time the arrangement of angels into three orders with three choirs in each (a legacy from the Pseudo-Dionysius) had come to be recognized: Seraphim, Cherubim, and Thrones, in the highest order; Dominations, Virtues, and Powers, in the second; and Principalities, Archangels, and Angels, in the lowest of the three orders. For biblical roots of this language, see Ephesians 1:21; 3:10; 6:12 and Colossians 1:16–20.

5. Wesley Carr, *Angels and Principalities: The Background, Meaning and Development of the Pauline Phrase* hai archai kai hai exousiai (Cambridge: Cambridge University Press, 1981).

6. Geddes MacGregor, *Gnosis* (Wheaton, Illinois: Theosophical Publishing House, 1979).

7. Rudolf Bultmann, *Theology of the New Testament* (tr. K. Grobel) Vol. I (New York: Charles Scribner's Sons, 1951), p. 170.

8. Bultmann, p. 171.

9. The entire section 15, "Gnostic Motifs" in Bultmann (pp. 164–183) is admirably enlightening on this vital question in New Testament scholarship. Gnostic themes abound also in the documents discovered in December 1945 and called the Nag Hammadi Library. See J. M. Robinson (ed.), *The Nag Hammadi Library*. (San Francisco: Harper & Row, 1977).

10. George Foot Moore, *Judaism* (Cambridge: Harvard University Press, 1927), Vol. 1, pp. 403 f.

11. The word *Shekhinah* does not occur in the Old Testament. It signifies "dwelling." It was sometimes used in rabbinical literature, however, as a sort of "stand-in" substitute for "God." For example, in the Targums (interpretations of the

Hebrew Bible made as an aid to synagogue worship) one finds (instead of "my eyes have looked at the King, Yahweh Sabaoth") the periphrasis: "my eyes have looked at the glory of the Shekhinah" (Isaiah 6:5). The New Testament writers occasionally echo this usage. A very striking example is in the Prologue to the Fourth Gospel: "The Logos was made flesh, he dwelt among us, and we saw his glory. . . ." (John 1:14). The juxtaposition of "glory" and "dwelling" is notable in that verse, which is of immense importance in traditional Christian liturgy and theology as a charter for the doctrine of the Incarnation.

12. I have discussed such distinctions in my book *Gnosis* (Wheaton, Illinois: Theosophical Publishing House, 1979).

13. The original texts suggest, rather, an indefinitely large number.

CHAPTER 5—SATAN: THE REALM OF ANGELS GONE WRONG

1. *Summa Theologiae,* I, qq. 62–64, especially q. 63.

2. For a detailed study of the renunciation and exorcism of the Devil in the numerous rites used in the Church in various places and throughout Christian history, see Henry Ansgar Kelly, *The Devil at Baptism: Ritual, Theology, and Drama* (Ithaca, New York: Cornell University Press, 1985). In this interesting and very scholarly work the author shows, *inter alia,* that exorcism is often missing in the earlier baptismal rites in the East.

3. Exorcism was fully recognized in Catholic tradition as a regular clerical function and might therefore sometimes be a clerical duty. The office of exorcist was one of the four "minor" orders conferred on candidates for the priesthood. It was abolished in the Roman Catholic Church in 1972.

4. For a discussion of the similarities and differences between Satan and Māra, see James W. Boyd, *Satan and Māra: Christian and Buddhist Symbols of Evil* (Leiden: E. J. Brill, 1975).

CHAPTER 6—LOVE AFFAIRS BETWEEN WOMEN AND FALLEN ANGELS

1. See Joseph Butler's celebrated *Analogy of Religion* (1736), Part I, Ch. 5.

CHAPTER 7—THE DEVELOPMENT OF OUR AWARENESS OF INVISIBLE HELPERS

1. John Macquarrie, *Principles of Christian Theology,* second edition (New York: Charles Scribner's Sons, 1966), pp. 233 ff.

2. Macquarrie, p. 234.

3. Macquarrie, p. 233. We should note, however, that the hierarchical nature of created being was recognized in the ninth century by Erigena as extending from "the highest angel" to "the lowest part of the rational and irrational soul," the part that is concerned with nutrition and growth. What the ancients and the medieval thinkers did not clearly see is that the hierarchy must be conceived as an evolutionary continuum. See his *De Divisione naturae,* Introduction. Nevertheless, an evolutionary principle is implicit even in Genesis I, for although in that account of creation God commands light to appear and light instantly does so, the creation of birds, fish, and other creatures takes several "days" and at the end of the process God takes a rest, a *šabbat.*

CHAPTER 8—PATRISTIC AND MEDIEVAL ANGELOLOGIES

1. *De Principiis,* I, 5, 1–3.

2. *Ibid.,* I, 6, 3.

3. *Ibid.,* I, 6, 4.

4. Enoch 40.

5. *De Principiis,* I, 8, 1.

6. *Ibid.,* I, 8.

7. *Ibid.,* II, 10, 7, and more especially, III, 2, 4.

8. *Ibid.,* III, 3, 4–6.

9. Ephesians 1:21; Colossians 1:16.

10. The mystical ascent, according to Pseudo-Dionysius, entails a process leading ultimately to the deification *(theiōsis)* of humanity. Such ideas of progressive deification, obtainable by a process of emptying the mind of both all reasoning activity and all sense perceptions, were more acceptable in Eastern than in Western Christianity. They offended the West's strong emphasis on the gulf that lies between the divine and the human. Christian mystics in the west, in the Benedictine, Spanish, and other mystical traditions drew, however, from the ideas handed down from the Pseudo-Dionysius, much of their notion of the soul's ascent to God, while cautiously avoiding, in most cases, the concept of deification. Some of the Spanish mystics, for instance, avoided it by specifying that even in the final rapture in which the soul is "married" to God, God and the soul are bound together by a cord of love *(hilo de amor):* a safeguard against the danger of any notion of deification of the human. Nevertheless, the model of mystical ascent to God is of notable importance for and relevance to what would be required to make sense of ancient and medieval constructs in terms of a modern evolutionary understanding of the universe.

11. *Summa Theologiae* I, q. 50, a. 1. See the entire treatise on the angels, *Ibid.,* I, qq. 50–64.

12. *Ibid.,* I, q. 50, a. 4.

13. *Ibid.,* I, q. 50, a. 5.

14. *Ibid.,* I, q. 51, a. 2.

15. *Ibid.,* I, q. 52, a. 1.

16. *Ibid.,* I, q. 52, a. 2.

17. *Ibid.,* I, q. 52, a. 3. This discussion may possibly have provided one of the sources for the popular belief that the schoolmen engaged in disputes about how many angels could dance on the point of a pin. We must understand that the question, as Thomas actually raises it, is a serious one in the medieval context and in terms of medieval forms of conceptualization. But see above, Chapter 2, note 3.

18. *De Civitate Dei* 11, 29.

19. *De spectaculis,* 30.

20. *Summa Theologiae* III, suppl., q. 94, a. 1.

CHAPTER 9—ANGELS IN LATER LITERATURE

1. *Institutes,* I, 14, 3.

2. In Calvin's time Moses was uncritically accepted, even by scholars, as the author of the Pentateuch, although it recounts his own death (Deuteronomy 34:5 f.)

3. *Institutes,* I, 14, 9. He renounces here the opinion attributed to the Sadducees (Acts 23:8) that angels do not exist except as human fancies.

4. I, 14, 4. Nevertheless, Calvin, when not preoccupied with systematic theologizing (in an exposition of Luke 16:22, for instance), writes as any Catholic might of "an unspeakably precious soul, carried by angels to a blessed life."

5. Henry Bullinger, *The Decades* (tr. H. I.) (Cambridge: The Parker Society, 1849–1852), col. 4, p. 388.

6. *The Chronicle of the English Augustinian Canonesses Regular of the Lateran,* ed. A. Hamilton (1904), I, pp. 251 f.

7. *Paradise Regained,* I, lines 131 ff.

8. Boehm, *Mysterium Magnum,* Chapter 8, section 28.

9. *Concerning the Earths in our Solar System,* section 79.

10. *Heaven and Its Wonders and Hell,* section 267.

11. *Heaven and Its Wonders and Hell,* ss. 234–242.

12. *Heaven and Its Wonders and Hell,* s. 230.

13. *Heaven and Its Wonders and Hell,* s. 229; II Samuel 24:17.

14. *Heaven and Its Wonders and Hell,* s. 602.

15. Ruysbroeck, *The Seven Steps of the Ladder of Spiritual Love,* (Westminster, London: Dacre Press, n.d.), p. 36.

16. F. Von Hügel, *The Mystical Element in Religion as Studied in Saint Catherine of Genoa and Her Friends* (London: J. M. Dent & Sons, 1927).

17. *Divine Names,* 4, 6.

18. *Celestial Hierarchy,* 4, 6. See Von Hügel, vol. 2, p. 97.

CHAPTER 12—ANGEL-LIKE BEINGS IN OTHER RELIGIONS

1. The dating of this early period of Indian literature is controversial, but most scholars place it between about 1500 and 1000 BCE.

2. On "Lucy," see Chapter 14.

CHAPTER 13—ARE ANGELS MERE FICTIONS OF THE RELIGIOUS IMAGINATION?

1. Demosthenes, *Third Olynthiac.*

2. Lucretius, *De rerum natura,* Book 5.

3. Statius, *Thebaid,* Book 3, line 664. His older contemporary, Petronius, makes a similar observation.

4. L. Feuerbach, *Das Wesen des Christentums,* preface to the second edition. In L. Feuerbach, *The Essence of Christianity,* trans. G. Eliot (New York: Harper Torchbooks, 1957), pp. xxxviii ff.

5. C. G. Jung, *Modern Man in Search of a Soul* (London: Routledge, 1933), p. 264.

6. C. G. Jung, *Psychological Types* (London: Routledge, 1923), p. 301.

7. C. G. Jung, *Symbols of Transformation* (New York: Harper Torchbooks, 1956), p. 348.

8. *Ibid.*

9. C. G. Jung, *Symbols of Transformation*, pp. 111–113.

10. *Ibid.*, p. 248.

11. *Ibid.*, p. 248, note 85.

CHAPTER 15—THE SUPERMAN IN ANCIENT AND MODERN THOUGHT

1. Genesis 18:23–33.

2. Epiphanius, *Panarion* XLVIII, 10.

CHAPTER 16—PARANORMAL EXPERIENCES SUCH AS COMMUNICATION WITH THE DEPARTED

1. F.W.H. Myers, *Human Personality and Its Survival of Bodily Death* (New Hyde Park, New York: University Books, Inc., 1961), Preface (by Susy Smith), p. 11.

2. S. Freud, *The Interpretation of Dreams* (tr. Brill; 3rd English edition, London: George Allen and Unwin, 1932), pp. 564 ff. We should note, in passing, that the notion that the psyche includes an area such as that which Freud delineated here was not new. Franz Delitzsch, for instance, writing in 1855, the year before Freud's birth, in *A System of Biblical Theology,* wrote that it had been "a fundamental error of most psychologists hitherto, to make the soul only extend so far as its consciousness extends; it embraces, as is now always acknowledged, a far greater abundance of powers and relations than can possibly appear in its consciousness."

3. From a poem by Frank Kendon, in *Arguments and Emblems* (London: The Bodley Head, Ltd., 1925), p. 76.

CHAPTER 17—ANGELS AS ANDROGYNS

1. See my *Reincarnation in Christianity* (Wheaton, Illinois: Theosophical Publishing House, 1978) and my *Reincarnation as a Christian Hope* (London: The Macmillan Press, 1982).

2. C. S. Lewis, *A Preface to Paradise Lost* (London: Oxford University Press, 1942).

3. Lewis, pp. 112–113. The passage in Lucretius to which Lewis refers is *De rerum natura,* IV, 1076–1111.

4. *Ibid.,* pp. 113–114.

CHAPTER 18—WHY ANGELS?

1. *Summa Theologiae,* I, 1, 9.

2. *Ibid.,* I, 46, 2.

3. *Ibid.,* I, 50, 1.

4. *Ibid.*

5. Psalm 90:4 (Jerusalem Bible).

6. *The Golden Book of Modern English Poetry, 1870–1920* (London and Toronto: Dent and Sons, 1927), p. 51.

BIBLIOGRAPHY

I. GENERAL SOURCES IN ENGLISH

Adler, Mortimer J. *The Angels and Us.* New York: Macmillan Publishing Co., Inc., 1982.
> An interesting and original study. Includes bibliographical references.

Alexandra, Illeana (Mother). *The Holy Angels.* Still River, MA: St. Bede's Publications, 1981.
> An Eastern Orthodox approach by the Abbess of the Orthodox monastery of the Transfiguration, Ellwood City, Pennsylvania, who is a daughter of King Ferdinand and Queen Marie of Romania. It contains an epilogue of her own personal experience of angels.

"Angel." *Encyclopedic Dictionary of the Bible* (New York: McGraw Hill, 1963), pp. 82–86.

"Angel." *The New International Dictionary of New Testament Theology.* (Gen. Ed., Colin Brown.) (Grand Rapids, MI: Zondervan, 1978), pp. 101–105.

"Angel." *The Oxford Dictionary of the Christian Church* (second edition), (New York: Oxford University Press, 1974), pp. 52 f.

"Angel of the Lord." *Encyclopedic Dictionary of the Bible* (New York: McGraw Hill, 1963), pp. 87 f.

"Angels and Angelology." *Encyclopaedia Judaica* (New York: Macmillan, 1971), pp. 955–976.

Anshen, Ruth N. *The Reality of the Devil.* New York: Harper and Row, 1972.

Bialas, A. A. "Angelology." *The New Catholic Encyclopedia* (New York: McGraw Hill, 1967), pp. 505 f.

Boros, Ladislaus. *Angels and Men.* New York: Seabury, 1976.

Boyd, James W. *Satan and Māra: Christian and Buddhist Symbols of Evil.* Leiden: E. J. Brill, 1975.
> A scholarly study.

Brandon, S.G.F. "Angels." *A Dictionary of Comparative Religion*. New York: Charles Scribner's Sons, 1970.
> A useful brief comparative outline of angels and their counterparts in major religions.

Collins, James D. *The Thomistic Philosophy of the Angels*. Washington, DC: Catholic University of America Press, 1947.

Daniélou, Jean. *The Angels and Their Mission*. Westminster, MD: Christian Classics, Inc., 1976.

Davidson, Gustav. *A Dictionary of Angels, Including the Fallen Angels*. New York: Macmillan (Free Press), 1967.
> Includes bibliography. A useful reference work, sometimes serious, sometimes tongue-in-cheek, always scholarly. Illustrated with valuable appendices and extensive bibliography.

Fallon, T. L. "Guardian Angels." *The New Catholic Encyclopedia* (New York: McGraw Hill, 1967), pp. 516–519.

Field, M. J. *Angels and Ministers of Grace*. New York: Hill and Wang, 1971.
> An interesting study. Dr. Field took her London Ph.D. in anthropology, then studied medicine, specialized in psychiatry, and worked in West African villages.

Freeman, Hobart E. *Angels of Light*. Plainfield, NJ: Logos International, 1969.

Gaebelin, A. C. *The Angels of God*. Grand Rapids, MI: Baker Book House, 1924.

Gaster, T. H. "Angel." *The Interpreter's Dictionary of the Bible*, I (New York: Abingdon, 1962), pp. 128–134.

Gilmore, G. Don. *Angels, Angels, Everywhere*. New York: Pilgrim Press, 1981.
> Includes bibliography.

Graham, William Franklin ("Billy"). *Angels: God's Secret Agents*. New York: Doubleday, 1975.
> This book, among the least thoughtful of Billy Graham's writings, is well known but cannot be recommended.

Hahn, Emily. *Breath of God*. Garden City, NY: Doubleday, 1971.

Hall, J. R. "Angels . . . and All the Holy Ones: The Dream of the Rood 153b –154a." *American Notes and Queries*, vol. XXIV, 5 and 6 (Jan.–Feb. 1986), pp. 65–68.
> A study of the question of angels in the Anglo-Saxon poem, *The Dream of the Rood*.

Hart, Rob van der. *Theology of Angels and Devils*. Cork, Ireland: The Mercier Press, 1973.

Hodson, Geoffrey. *Brotherhood of Angels and of Men.* London: Theosophical Publishing House, 1973.

Holden, Ursula. *Fallen Angels.* New York: Methuen, 1979.

Jung, Leo. *Fallen Angels in Jewish and Christian and Mohammedan Literature.* New York: Ktav Publishing House, 1926.

Kelly, Henry A. *The Devil at Baptism: Ritual, Theology, and Drama.* Ithaca, NY: Cornell University Press, 1985.
> A definitive study of the role of the Devil in the baptismal rite of both Eastern and Western liturgies.

Leadbeatter, C. W. *Invisible Helpers.* Adyar, India: Theosophical Publishing House, 1956.

Lewis, C. S. *A Preface to Paradise Lost.* London: Oxford University Press, 1942.

Lewis, C. S. *The Screwtape Letters.* London: Geoffrey Bles, 1942.
> Imaginary and highly provocative letters from a senior devil to his apprentice on the art of tempting humans.

MacDonald, D. B. "Malā'ika." *The Encyclopedia of Islam.* Leiden: E. J. Brill, 1936.
> The word is the Arabic broken plural of an early Semitic, possibly Canaanite, word *mal'ak,* meaning "messenger."

Maritain, Jacques. *The Sin of the Angel: An Essay on a Re-interpretation of Some Thomistic Positions.* Westminster, MD: Newman Press, 1959.
> Some bibliographical references.

Matter, E. Ann. "Angel/Angelology." *Dictionary of the Middle Ages.* New York: Scribner, 1982.

McKenzie, John L. "Angel." *Dictionary of the Bible* (Milwaukee, WI: The Bruce Publishing Company, 1965), pp. 30–33.

Moltmann, Jürgen. *The Future of Creation.* Philadelphia: Fortress Press, 1979.
> A collection of essays, many of them relevant to the central theme of the present study; one of them is on creation as an open system.

Newhouse, Flower A. *Rediscovering the Angels.* Wheaton, IL.: Theosophical Publishing House, 1986.
> By a theosophical clairvoyant. 17 full-page illustrations.

O'Donoghue, Noël Dermot. *The Holy Mountain: Approaches to the Mystery of Prayer.* Dublin: Michael Glazier, Ltd., 1983.
> Although this collection of pieces, very Celtic in spirit, by an Irish Discalced Carmelite priest, is not entirely relevant to a study of angelology, it contains an interesting chapter on angels in the course of a deeply spiritual series of studies.

Patterson, Robert M. *The Angels and Their Ministrations.* Philadelphia: Westminster Press, 1900.

Peterson, Erik. *The Angels and the Liturgy.* New York: Herder and Herder, 1964. Translation of *Das Buch von der Engeln.*

Raine, Kathleen. *Blake and Tradition.* Princeton: Princeton University Press, 1968. Bollingen Series XXXV.11. The A. W. Mellon Lectures in the Fine Arts, 1962. The National Gallery of Art, Washington, D.C.
    Contains many allusions to angels and related subject with copious illustrations, some of them Blake's.

Régamey, Raymond. *What Is an Angel?* New York: Hawthorn Books, 1960.
    Includes bibliography.

Riedl, John O. "The Nature of the Angels." Robert E. Brennan, O.P. (ed.), *Essays in Thomism.* New York: Sheed and Ward, 1942, pp. 113–148.

Ross, George MacDonald. "Angels." *Philosophy,* 60:234 (October 1985), pp. 495–511.
    A study by a contemporary philosopher raising some interesting questions about the meaning of the concept of angels in traditional usage.

Russell, Jeffrey Burton. *Lucifer: The Devil in the Middle Ages.* Ithaca, NY: Cornell University Press, 1984.
    A scholarly study by a specialist in diabology. Contains interesting illustrations, some of them unusual.

Sheed, F. J. (ed.). *Soundings in Satanism.* New York: Sheed and Ward, 1972.
    A collection of articles varying in quality but generally interesting and including one by J. -K Hysmans on the "Black Mass."

Sumrall, Lester F. *The Reality of Angels.* Nashville, TN: T. Nelson, 1982.

Swedenborg, E. *Angelic Wisdom Concerning the Divine Love and Wisdom.* London: The Swedenborg Society, 1969.
    A classic exposition of Swedenborg's teaching.

Tsuji, S. "Angels." *The New Catholic Encyclopedia* (New York: McGraw Hill, 1967), pp. 506–516.

Ward, Theodore. *Men and Angels.* New York: Viking Press, 1969.
    A thoughtful study, interestingly illustrated.

Waters, Clara Clement. *Angels in Art.* Boston: L. C. Page, 1906.

West, R. H. *Milton and the Angels.* Athens, GA: Georgia University Press, 1955.

Wilson, J. M. "Angel." *The International Standard Bible Encyclopedia* (Grand Rapids, MI: Eerdmans, 1979), pp. 124–127.

Wilson, Peter Lamborn. *Angels.* London: Thames and Hudson, 1980.

Wulfing, Sulamith. *Angels.* Werkerke, Holland, 1980.

Wulfing, Sulamith. *Witches, Goblins, and the Other World.* Werkerke, Holland, 1980.

II. SOME STANDARD FRENCH AND GERMAN SOURCE MATERIALS

Andres, F. *Die Engellehre der griechischen Apologeten des II Jahrh. und ihr Verhältnis zur griechische-römischen Dämonologie (Forschungen zum christ. Literatur und Dogmengeschichte, XII).* Paderborn, 1914.
    Contains extensive bibliography, pp. xi–xx.

Andres, F. "Die Engels—und Dämonenlehre des Clemens von Alexandrien." *Römische Quartalschrift,* 34 (1926), pp. 13–27; 129–40; 307–29.

Bareille, G. "Angélologie d'après les Pères." *Dictionnaire de théologie catholique* I, cols. 1192–1222.

Baumgart, Hildegard. *Der Engel in der modernen spanischen Literatur.* Geneva: Droz, 1958.

Duhr, J. "Anges." *Dictionnaire de spiritualité ascétique et mystique, doctrine et histoire,* cols. 586 ff.

Frey, J. B. "L'angélologie juive au temps de Jésus-Christ." Revue des Sciences philosophiques et théologiques, 5 (1911), pp. 75–110.

Gorceix, Bernard. "L'Ange en Allemagne au XVIIe siecle." *Recherches Germaniques,* 7 (1977), pp. 3–28.
    A learned and most interesting study with special reference to Boehme and Scheffler.

Hackspill, L. "L' Angélologie juive à l'époque néotestamentaire." *Revue Biblique* 11 (1902), pp. 527–550.

Hammerstein, Reinhold. *Diabolus in Musica: Studien zur Ikonographie der Musik im Mittelalter.* Bern: Francke Verlag, 1974.

Hofmann, K. "Engel." J. Höfer and K. Rahner (eds.), *Lexikon für Theologie und Kirche.* Freiburg, 1959.

Krauss, Johann Ulrich. *Biblisches Engel- u. Kunstwerck.* Facsimile reprint of the original edition (1694). Portland, OR: Collegium Graphicum, n.d.

Kurz, L. *Gregors des Grossen Lehre von den Engeln.* Rome, 1938.

Kurze, G. *Der Engels- und Taufelsglaube des Apostels Paulus.* Freiburg im Breisgau, 1915.

Lemonnyer, A. "Angélologie." *Dictionnaire de la Bible* (suppl.) cols. 255–262. Ed. L. Pirot. Paris: Letouzey et Ane, 1928 ff.

Müller, Caspar Detlef Gustav. *Die Engellehre der koptischen Kirche.* Wiesbaden: O. Harrassowitz, 1959.

Pelz, K. *Die Engellehre des hl. Augustinus.* Münster, 1913.

Peterson, E. *Das Buch von den Engeln. Stellung und Bedeutung der hl. Engel im Kultus.* Leipzig, 1935.
    English tr.: *The Angels and the Liturgy.*

Régamey, R. *Anges.* Paris: P. Tisné, 1946.

Schade, Herbert. "Zum Bild des Engels in der modernen Kunst." *Geist und Leben* (August 1973. 46 Jahrgang Heft 4), pp. 283–299. Echter Verlag Würzburg.

Touzard, J. "Ange de Jahvé." *Dictionnaire de la Bible* (1928), I, cols. 242–55. Ed. F. Vigouroux. Paris: Letouzey et Ane (5 vols.) 1895–1912.

Turmel, J. "Histoire de l'angélologie des temps apostoliques à la fin du cinquième siecle." *Revue d'histoire et de littérature religieuse,* 3–4 (1898–99), pp. 289 ff., 407 ff., 533 ff.

Vacant, A. "Ange." *Dictionnaire de la Bible* (suppl.), I, cols. 576–590. Ed. L. Pirot. Paris: Letouzey et Ane, 1928 ff.

Vacant, A. "Angélologie dans l'Eglise latine depuis le temps des Pères jusqu'à Saint Thomas." *Dictionnaire de théologie catholique,* I, cols. 1222 ff. Ed. A. Vacant, E. Mangenot, and E. Amann. Paris: Letouzey et Ane (15 vols.), 1903–1950.

Vacant, A. "Angélologie de Saint Thomas d'Aquin et des scolastiques postérieurs." *Dictionnaire de théologie catholique,* I, cols. 1228 ff. Ed. A. Vacant, E. Mangenot, and E. Amann. Paris: Letouzey et Ane (15 vols.), 1903–1950.

Wilmart, A. "Prières à l 'Ange Gardien." *Auteurs spirituels du moyen age latin* (Paris, 1932), pp. 537–58.

III. SOME ANCIENT, MEDIEVAL, AND REFORMATION SOURCES

Aquinas, Thomas. *Summa Theologiae,* I, qq. 50–56.

Aquinas, Thomas. *Tractatus de substantiis separatis.* West Hartford, CT: St. Joseph College, 1962.
> The Latin text based on twelve medieval manuscripts.

Augustine. *De civitate Dei,* XI, XII.

Bonaventure. *Breviloquium,* II, sections 6–8.

Calvin, John. *Institutes,* I, 3–19. *Calvin: Institutes of the Christian Religion.* (Philadelphia: Westminster Press, 1940), vol. 1, pp. 162–178.

Dionysius (Pseudo-). *Celestial Hierarchy (Peri tēs ouranias hierarchias).*

Luther, Martin. *Table Talk. Luther's Works,* vol. 54. Philadelphia: Fortress Press, 1967.

Moses Maimonides. *Guide for the Perplexed,* 4–7; 12–13; 49.

Origen. *De principiis,* II, 9; III, 5–6.

Suarez, F. *Summa Theologiae de rerum omnium creatore, II. De Angelis.* Lyon, 1620.

INDEX

Boldface page numbers indicate illustrations.